The Talk of the Town

The Bucknell Studies in Eighteenth-Century Literature and Culture

The Bucknell Studies in Eighteenth-Century Literature and Culture aims to publish challenging, new eighteenth-century scholarship. Of particular interest is critical, historical, and interdisciplinary work that is interestingly and intelligently theorized, and that broadens and refines the conception of the field. At the same time, the series remains open to all theoretical perspectives and different kinds of scholarship. While the focus of the series is the literature, history, arts, and culture (including art, architecture, music, travel, and history of science, medicine, and law) of the long eighteenth century in Britain and Europe, the series is also interested in scholarship that establishes relationships with other geographies, literature, and cultures for the period 1660–1830.

Titles in This Series

Juliette Cherbuliez, *The Place of Exile: Leisure Literature and the Limits of Absolutism*
Tita Chico, *Designing Women: The Dressing Room in Eighteenth-Century English Literature and Culture*
Dan Doll and Jessica Munns, ed., *Recording and Reordering: Essays on the Seventeenth- and Eighteenth-Century Diary and Journal*
Ziad Elmarsafy, *Freedom, Slavery, and Absolutism: Corneille, Pascale, Racine*
Regina Hewitt and Pat Rogers, eds., *Orthodoxy and Heresy in Eighteenth-Century Society*
Susan Paterson Glover, *Engendering Legitimacy: Law, Property, and Early Eighteenth-Century Fiction*
Catherine Jones, *Literary Memory: Scott's Waverley Novels and the Psychology of Narrative*
Sarah Jordan, *The Anxieties of Idleness: Idleness in Eighteenth-Century British Literature and Culture*
Deborah Kennedy, *Helen Maria Williams and the Age of Revolution*
Chris Mounsey, *Christopher Smart: Clown of God*
Chris Mounsey, ed., *Presenting Gender: Changing Sex in Early Modern Culture*
Frédéric Ogée, ed., *"Better in France?": The Circulation of Ideas across the Channel in the Eighteenth Century*
Roland Racevskis, *Time and Ways of Knowing Under Louis XIV: Molière, Sévigné, Lafayette*
Laura Rosenthal and Mita Choudhury, eds., *Monstrous Dreams of Reason*
Katherine West Scheil, *The Taste of the Town: Shakespearian Comedy and the Early Eighteenth-Century Theater*
Philip Smallwood, ed., *Johnson Re-Visioned: Looking Before and After*
Peter Walmsley, *Locke's* Essay *and the Rhetoric of Science*
Lisa Wood, *Modes of Discipline: Women, Conservatism, and the Novel after the French Revolution*
Mark Blackwell, ed., *The Secret Life of Things: Animals, Objects, and It-Narratives in Eighteenth-Century England*
Evan Gottlieb, *Feeling British: Sympathy and National Identity in Scottish and English Writing, 1701–1832*
http://www.bucknell.edu/universitypress/

The Talk of the Town

Figurative Publics in Eighteenth-Century Britain

Ann C. Dean

Lewisburg
Bucknell University Press

Associated University Presses
2010 Eastpark Boulevard
Cranbury, NJ 08512

The paper used in this publication meets the requirements of the American National Standard for Permanence of Paper for Printed Library Materials Z39.48-1984.

Library of Congress Cataloging-in-Publication Data

Dean, Ann C., 1967–
The talk of the town : figurative publics in eighteenth-century Britain / Ann C. Dean.
p. cm.
Includes bibliographical references and index.
ISBN-13: 978-0-8387-5672-0 (alk. paper)
ISBN-10: 0-8387-5672-7 (alk. paper)
1. Great Britain—Intellectual life—18th century. 2. Discourse analysis—Social aspects—Great Britain—History—18th century. 3. Public opinion—Great Britain—History—18th century. 4. Press and politics—Great Britain—History—18th century. 5. Coffeehouses—Great Britain—Social aspects. 6. Great Britain—Civilization—18th century. 7. Press—Great Britain—Influence—History—18th century. I. Title.

DA485.D43 2007
941.07—dc22 2006034649

PRINTED IN THE UNITED STATES OF AMERICA

Contents

Acknowledgments 7

Introduction 11

1. Figuring Coffehouse Talk in the *Spectator* and Its Heirs 25
2. Creating a Clamor: The Language of Court Politics 46
3. Clamor in the Newspapers: Figurative Publics in Midcentury Newspaper Writing 74
4. Candid Debate: Representing Parliamentary Procedure 100

Epilogue: Figurative Publics and Revolutionary Discourse 127

Notes 133

Bibliography 140

Index 144

Acknowledgments

A PARADE OF GENEROUS, BRILLIANT, AND KIND PEOPLE CHALLENGED and supported me as I worked on this project. It is a pleasure to be able to print and circulate an image of the gratitude I feel so strongly.

In graduate school, where I began to work on these ideas, I benefited from studying with scholars whose questions provoked me to return repeatedly to these texts. My debt to Michael Warner's work will be clear to any reader of this study; I would also like to thank Myra Jehlen, Bruce Robbins, Michael McKeon, and Richard Miller. Other readers also intervened crucially in my shaping of the manuscript: Stephanie Volmer, Kara Donaldson, Kathy Ashley, Ruth Dean, Terri Nickel, David Collings, and the anonymous reader for Bucknell University Press.

For emotional, logistical, financial, and recreational support in various combinations, I would like to thank my family: Jonathan, Ruth, Alex, and Melissa Dean and Anne, Martin, Rozzie, and Margaret Hayden; the poker group: Vic Tulli, Stephanie Volmer, Kathy Crown, Kevil Duhon, Matthew Shifman, Cora Turlish, Jennifer and Dario Arena, Takashi Yokoyama, and Jay Stevenson; Tomas and Marilu Fortson and the Bowdoin squash community; Carol Bork; Tanya Agathocleous; Nancy Abelmann; Priti Joshi; Allison Basile; Vineet Shende; Hillary Brown; and Ann Flannery.

My husband, Bernardo Feliciano, burned himself to a crisp teaching middle school science for the eight years it took me to earn my PhD and is taking care of our daughter Nelle as I write these words. His gifts of intelligence, time, and love have made this project possible.

A portion of chapter 2 was published in *ELH* 73 (2006): 631–49.

The Talk of the Town

Introduction

What does a good political discussion sound like? How can that sound be represented in print? The intellectual work of imagining a public engaged in such discussions is central to the development of republican government. Informed public opinion is developed, according to theorists including Immanuel Kant and Jürgen Habermas, through a universally accessible process of discussion carried on according to universally applicable rules of reason. Over the course of the eighteenth century, British writers frequently reported that they had participated in such discussions, often locating them in spaces that were neither universally accessible nor reasonable—private parties, male-only urban coffee houses, the king's Drawing Room. This study argues that in eighteenth-century Britain the public sphere was a figure of speech created through juxtaposed images of more limited, local, and particular arenas of discussion. In letters, newspapers, and books, eighteenth-century British writers described the "public" qualities of three different spaces: court, coffeehouse, and Parliament. Writers metaphorically abstracted the qualities of these social spaces, describing the nation's many coffeehouses, drawing rooms, and meetings and the customary language that circulated among them.

This universalizing move allowed writers to describe people not physically in a space as participating in its customary habits and activities. Thus "coffee-house talk," by midcentury, referred not only to particular conversations in particular coffeehouses, but also to a general understanding that such conversations were taking place and to the representation of those conversations in other conversations, in letters, and in newspapers and books. Women reading the *Public Advertiser* beside a fireplace in Scotland, or tradesmen reading old copies of the *Spectator* in Philadelphia, might thus understand their reading, thinking, and conversation in terms of "coffeehouse talk." The coffeehouse itself became a metaphor for a particular kind of sociable interaction, just as our current use of the word "forum" suggests a particular courtyard in Rome to indicate the concept of the open political discussion that was sometimes practiced there.

A second metaphor recasts the sounds of gossip heard in another space, the king's Drawing Room, as a vehicle for "clamour heard everywhere," a sound representing the complaints and demands of powerful family alliances competing for patronage and favor. Thirdly, late in the century, the details of debates in the House of Commons became available in weekly newspapers. Abstracting the representative qualities of the House, writers associated activities such as proposing motions and taking votes with "candid debate" as a universally available practice.

To understand the interactions among court, coffeehouse, and Parliament as figurative spaces, it is necessary to distinguish between empirical accounts of political conversation and metaphors derived from the significance of those discussions. It is quite different to report on a conversation one has overheard than to claim that "everyone is saying" something or that the "voice of the people" has enunciated it. The first is a literal reference, the second a generalization, and the third a metaphor. The political effects of these different uses of language are clear in a letter to the *London Chronicle* printed August 1, 1765. Defending the current administration, the writer claimed that "the new Ministry . . . are called to the helm by the united voice of the K— —, the R— —, F— —, and the people." In this case, the new ministers had literally been "called" by the individual voice of the king, who invited them to take their offices and kiss his hands in front of his court. The figurative language at work here becomes clear if one tries to imagine the sound of his voice "united" with those of the "R[oyal] F[amily]" and "the people." What would that sound like? In what space would it be heard? The united voice is a figure for the King's role as representative of the people and of their loyalty to him (and not to any particular faction or influential individual).

The united voice is a common metaphor in eighteenth-century political writing, one that derives from oral language just as the metaphor "clear as the ABC" derives from print. Scholars working on print culture and the history of the book have described such figurations: to be "in print" in Western modernity signifies clarity, accessibility, and social approval. Oral and manuscript media were available for the same set of textual uses: literal reference, generalization, and figuration.[1] By separating writers' *uses of* media to circulate their works from the *references to* those media as metaphors for communication itself, we can see how figurative language structures eighteenth-century descriptions of public political discussion. Print became a useful concept for thinking about audience, circulation, and argument when writers turned it into a trope, as they had done earlier with other media such as conversations and letters. A helpful example can be found in a letter Horace Walpole addressed to his friend Horace Mann on March 26, 1769. Mann was in Florence serving as an ambassador, and Walpole kept him up to date on political and social events:

> Our ministers, like their Saxon ancestors, are gone to hold a Witenagemot on horseback at Newmarket. Lord Chatham, we are told, is to come forth after the holidays and place himself at the head of the discontented. When I see it, I shall believe it.
>
> Lord Frederick Campbell is at last to be married this evening to the Dowager Countess of Ferrers. The Duchess of Grafton is actually Countess Ossory. This is a short gazette; but consider, it is a time of truce.[2]

To describe either a culture of print or a culture of public discussion, it is important to make distinctions between any writer's use of a technology as a medium, in the way Walpole here uses manuscript; as a metaphor, in the way Walpole here uses print; or in a literal description, in the way Walpole here uses oral gossip. By referring to his letter as a gazette, Walpole compares it to the printed newssheet issued with government approval, which listed marriages, bankruptcies, offices taken up and resigned, and court events. The medium for this letter was manuscript—Walpole did not offer it for print during his lifetime. Print is not a medium here but a metaphor for the communication of the news of the day—a "short gazette." Walpole also makes a literal reference to orality as a medium by reporting what "we are told" around the card and dinner tables of the people eager to claim an association with the popular but reclusive William Pitt. Walpole, whose manuscript letters fill thirty-six volumes, also ran a private printing press at his country house, Strawberry Hill. His use of all three media in his social and political life is perhaps especially noticeable but not unrepresentative of his contemporaries.

Walpole's manuscript gazette provides a characteristic example of the importance of figuration in eighteenth-century descriptions of political discourse and ideas. It is difficult to interpret the writing in political letters and newspapers without understanding the ways that the media themselves could become metaphors. The situation is further complicated by another group of metaphors or figures, those based on spaces. In this series of figures, coffeehouses, drawing rooms, and meetings took on metaphorical resonance abstracted from particular places.

These figures were employed with special dexterity and influence by the writers of the *Spectator,* who described Mr. Spectator as a wanderer in the city and used the conversation overheard in public places as a framing device for introducing topics: "Last Night, upon my going into a Coffee-House not far from the Hay-Market Theatre, I diverted my self for above half an Hour with overhearing the Discourse. . . ."[3] Mr. Spectator's rambles from one place "of general resort" to another popularized this way of figuring those spaces as multiple and of treating that multiplicity as significant and representative.[4] Fifty years later, newspapers were still making frequent use of references to coffeehouses as multiple and as related by circulating discourse. The *London Chronicle* printed a poem entitled "The Moralist" on October 17, 1765. Arguing for a reformation of morals, the poet urged readers:

> Let coffee-house talk be no longer low chatt'rings
> Or intentional arguments raise;
> Or politics e'er be attended with flatt'rings
> Or no statesman have more than due praise.

This stanza pairs courtly extravagance with urban sociability, treating both as examples of the debased discourse of the times. The linguistic forms, chattering and flattering, are here equated with the space of the coffeehouse as representative of the temper of the times. The poem does not indicate a particular coffeehouse, but implies that a recognizable coffeehouse talk might be found at any of the city's more than five hundred establishments.[5] Like the *Spectator* writers, many political commentators used this convention as a familiar way to introduce their pieces. In September a correspondent to the same paper began a piece by characterizing "this time of political rage, [when] coffee-houses swarm with disputants for each party . . ."[6]

These conventional references use familiar spaces and familiar forms of language to create figures carrying complex significance. Figurations such as "coffee-house talk," "clamor" in the drawing rooms of courtiers, or "free and candid debate" in a civic meeting referred to three phenomena: replicated spaces, the language practiced in those spaces and circulated among them, and an awareness of replication and circulation as general social phenomena. Each figure, then, derived part of its meaning from its place among the others. The juxtaposition of figures, in adjoining columns of a newspaper or adjacent paragraphs in a letter, indicated a particular figure's part in the larger system of replication and circulation.

Eighteenth-century writers frequently commented on the replication of space in British cities. Coffeehouses were springing up among the other places of amusement and general resort. The court was surrounded by houses and clubs where politicians and courtiers met to strategize. Coffeehouses, assembly rooms, and taverns were patronized by the many voluntary societies in which citizens met to engage in civic life. Each of these spaces was associated with particular forms of conversation, and many writers followed the *Spectator* in recording and commenting upon those forms.

Writing itself shared in creating the sense that discourse was circulating among those replicated spaces. A bon mot might be repeated from table to table in a single coffeehouse, then later at dinner, and again the next day over tea and at yet more coffeehouses. It might also be recorded in letters and diaries and sometimes find its way into a newspaper or pamphlet. A self-reflexive awareness of these capacities for replication and circulation meant that each of these phrases (coffeehouse talk, clamor, and candid debate) referred to its own abstraction. Each phrase refers to any particular conversation as one of many, part of a system of spaces among which talk can circulate and be replicated and of media for replicating and circulating it. The accumulated amount of talk taking place was important to eighteenth-century writers, whether they referred to it negatively as "chatt'rings" or positively as sociable conversation or intelligent discussion.

Accumulation gave this talk significance. Such figurations are central to imagining a group of people as a public, defined by Michael Warner as "a body of strangers united through the circulation of their discourse."[7] A newspaper's comment on generalized coffeehouse talk poses that talk, and its own comment upon it, as meaningful in relation to other conversations and writing. These ideas became a conceptual struture for organizing and understanding social life. A particular conversation can only draw on this significance if it is one of many and if it can be repeated and circulated among the others, retold at another sociable meal later in the day, written in a letter, or printed in a pamphlet, newspaper, or book.

The newspapers and letters examined in this study do not describe a single, enormous, bounded community resembling the nationalist consciousness analyzed by Benedict Anderson—one huge coffeehouse.[8] Instead, writers describe hundreds of coffeehouses with people and language circulating among them. Both literally and figuratively, then, such a space is replicated. Like the powerful image of replicated typeset pages providing the clarity of the ABC, the image of replicated spaces invests descriptions of conversation with political significance. When described in this way, an exchange or witticism is significant not just in its own context, but in a wider arena where other such comments are being made, repeated, and circulated. The habits of conversation associated with a particular space circulate outside that space, increasing access to the conventions of that space.

Our spatial language for these phenomena suggests the need for an image to ground the concept of public discourse. We need a sense that there are boundaries, edges that define a space and thus connect the participants. It is for this reason that we still use a spatial term to describe publicity—the sphere. Jürgen Habermas's history of the term "public sphere" explains the usefulness of the concept in just this way. Inside a public sphere of discussion, participants are united by their agreement on rationality and the desirability of the public good. Their discourse is addressed, inside this sphere, to each other. There are listeners as well as speakers. There is the possibility of communication and of change.[9]

We are so accustomed to this figure of speech, the public sphere, that it is difficult to disentangle the substitution at the heart of it. When a citizen writes a letter to the editor, for instance, she addresses "the public." Her words are typeset, printed in multiple copies of the newspaper, distributed to houses and businesses, read or ignored, and disposed of. A few copies might find their ways into attics, libraries, or archives. Some copies might be passed from hand to hand. Her letter might be clipped, reprinted, sent to new readers in the mail, or posted on a bulletin board. It might provoke response from other readers. A map of the movement of the letter writer's words would contain multiple branching lines, some longer, some perhaps doubling back on themselves. Where then is an entity, the public? What is spherical?

It is important to the concept of republican government that we connect individual readers. They are not consumers or existentially isolated individuals or members of a clan; they are members of the public. Unifying them in that way produces a sense of boundedness, a three-dimensional image rather than a series of lines. Habermas's sphere, then, is a metaphor as much as the *Spectator*'s coffeehouse is. I argue that although eighteenth-century writers often referred to single, bounded groups such as the nation or the people, they did not describe these entities as spheres *of discussion.* Political talk was located, instead, in multiple, replicated spaces: representative coffeehouses, drawing rooms, or meetings. Figures created from these spaces indicated a more abstract sense of conversation as public, while still deriving from familiar spaces and daily conversations.

In making these observations, I am intervening in a conversation about Habermas's work that focuses on the problems caused by defining the public sphere as a "category of bourgeois society" allied to property ownership and middle-class decorum. Nancy Fraser's work with Habermas's ideas begins from the premise that "the general idea of the public sphere is indispensable to critical theory," but that "the specific form in which Habermas has elaborated this idea is not wholly satisfactory." Because Habermas stops short of "developing a new, postbourgeois model of the public sphere," his ideas are limiting for feminists and others who need conceptual tools for critical political work. She argues for the democratic potential of "the proliferation of a multiplicity of competing publics," which would provide opportunities for debate and action in a variety of modes, according to a variety of standards of decorum, legitimacy, and value.[10] Eighteenth-century newspaper descriptions of public discussion provide an angle of view for people engaged in finding and exploiting such opportunities. Not only are multiple public spheres identifiable in these texts, I argue; they are inevitable and constitutive. Even the aristocratic and bourgeois publics I examine in this study imagined themselves in the spaces between multiple conversations and acts of reading.

The *Public Advertiser* printed two pieces using characteristic juxtaposed figures of public speech in its issue of April 25, 1771. In adjacent columns, writers made contrasting claims about the political significance of sounds heard around the city. A civic association had held a dinner and procession in support of newspaper printers then being prosecuted by the House of Commons for printing accounts of its debates. Writing in support of the government, "Piso" dismisses the group's actions, claiming that "in the Clamour against the House of Commons, the Voice of the People did not join the Noise of factious Men." The distinction between these two sounds is vital. The complaints that can be heard echoing in the streets are significant, according to Piso, only as evidence of the power of faction. The more abstract voice that represents the public good has not joined in. The only sound to be heard, then, is noise.

An entirely different figure based on the same sound is presented in the same issue's news reports. Describing the same "factious men" Piso so disapproves of, the newswriter reports that "the Number of Persons who flocked from all the neighbouring Parts, and the repeated loud Shouts of Applause, during that long Procession, were never exceeded. The People seemed to have only one Heart and one Voice." As in Piso's letter, this report uses a figure of repeated, echoing sound to suggest a generalized political sentiment. "Clamour" and "repeated loud shouts" both present public opinion as a phenomenon imaginable in the spaces between echoing utterances. The difference of opinion between the two writers is over the motivations behind that opinion: is it a view promulgated by a small self-interested group or a conclusion reached by considering the good of the whole? Is it a voice or a noise? By juxtaposing these contradictory figures, the printed page of the *Public Advertiser* indicates possibilities that neither writer acknowledges: perhaps the difference of opinion can be analyzed and judged against evidence. Perhaps political discourse can be both divided and virtuous. If political sounds are significant only when they echo and repeat, then juxtaposing figures of "united voices" allows for difference.

This study does not present a narrative of development or a genealogy of a single concept such as "the political nation." Instead it presents a set of interrelated, competing, and mutually defining metaphors and figurations. Identifying the relations between these metaphors requires work in an archive that crosses the boundaries of court, coffeehouse, and Parliament and between manuscript and print. Letters and memoirs written by court figures such as Horace Walpole, the Grenville and Temple families, Edmund Burke, and King George III describe oral interchanges at court of which we have no other record, and present evidence of the institutions and conventions for creating and circulating writing in manuscript. Read in conjunction with these materials, London's weekly newspapers can be seen to draw on oral and manuscript conventions and figures. They also develop new conventions and figures for their own medium, print, many derived from the influential work of the *Spectator* writers. I have concentrated on the *London Chronicle* and *Public Advertiser,* both of which published material sympathetic to reform and suspicious of the state as well as defenses of various ministries and measures.

The newspapers of this period are full of images of eavesdroppers in the king's Drawing Room, coffeehouse loungers with time on their hands, and upstanding members of civic associations. My reading is focused on the period between the Seven-Years' War and the American

Revolution, when a series of issues gave newspapers opportunities to characterize their readers, as well as to address them. The terms of the Peace of Paris, which ended the Seven Years' War, provoked widespread frustration, particularly at King George III's favorite, John Stuart, the third Earl of Bute. The eight changes of administration between 1760 and 1770 released tides of speculation and gossip as courtiers negotiated for alliances and jockeyed for position. John Wilkes was arrested for libel under a general warrant in 1763 and expelled from the House of Commons in 1769, and in response crowds, newspaper readers and writers, and gossips complained, argued, and speculated. In the American colonies, developing resistance to taxation produced similar effects. And during the entire period, newspaper printers repeatedly went to jail for circulating accounts of Parliament's debates.

In newspaper reports on and discussions of these events, figures based on courtly politics were used to describe the popular agitation over John Wilkes; figures based on sound were used to describe newspaper reports; figures based on newspapers were used to describe oral negotiations. Tropes on one medium appeared in writing generated in another. By following figures from one medium to another, and by examining the contexts in which they were used, it is possible to see a social imaginary emerging from the juxtapositions between figures. When columns on the same page of a newspaper denounced clamor and praised applause, those figurations began to refer to each other in an abstract arena of circulating discourse itself. Only in such juxtapositions did these writers gesture toward a public sphere.

Considering the significance of figures in and of newspapers addresses a problem raised by historians of the newspaper press in the eighteenth century. Large-scale historical narratives suggest that the growth of weekly papers and the availability of political news contributed to the growing interest in republican thought, popular participation in politics, and eventually to the war in America and electoral reform in Britain. Establishing the way this contribution worked, however, has been difficult. Few studies have worked closely with the texts of the papers themselves; in those that have, the connection between newspapers and political change has been difficult to identify. In his account of political news in eighteenth-century papers, for instance, Jeremy Black has claimed that rather than presenting a critical audience before which the ancien régime state was forced to legitimate itself, as Habermas argues, newspapers simply provided new space for the conduct of political business as usual: "in many senses the press and the amorphous pressures, interests and opinions understood by the term public opinion were part of the political system itself."[11] Hannah Barker does see the newspapers helping to "define[] the public and public opinion in ways which were increasingly broad and which were credited with greater influence in the nation's political life and structure." She places this development, however, quite late in the century, "between 1779 and 1785," at which point weekly newspapers had been familiar in London for seventy years and cheap, printed, political commentary for closer to a century.[12] Both writers claim that, despite the work of Elizabeth Eisenstein and Habermas, more work is needed with specific newspapers to test and refine the larger historical narratives proposed by these scholars and their critics. This study takes up that invitation by arguing that newspapers provided space in which figures could be juxtaposed. It was in adjacent columns that figures drawn from gossip interacted with figures drawn from print or from manuscript and in which metaphors based on the court ran into those based on the coffeehouse or the parliamentary meeting. Newspapers did not serve as a transparent medium for transmitting political ideas or for developing new ones. Instead, newspapers themselves became figures. As media, they provided space for a series of other figures through which writers imagined and reimagined political conversation.

Questions about the specific role of newspapers are set within the larger frame of historical work on political culture outside of the government and the social elites who made up the court and Parliament. Historians have extensively studied crowds, civic associations, and "out-of-doors political culture" in the period.[13] These studies, however, often borrow the language of the period and treat these groups as speaking only with the "united voice of the people." Kathleen Wilson's study of popular nationalism during the period, for instance, reveals the primacy of such images of unity and unanimity in popular political culture.[14] Like the historical work with newspapers, these studies raise an important question—how was it possible, in the eighteenth century, to imagine members of the public talking *to each other?* The work of Wilson and her colleagues makes it clear that they did. But, interestingly, eighteenth-century writers themselves did not represent such conversations as accessible and rational, as in the model presented by Habermas and Kant. The people "gathered from many parts" who were described in the *Public Advertiser* as having "only one voice" were, by definition, unable to talk among themselves, to judge competing arguments, to refine their views. Some coffeehouse and street-corner conversations may have been rational, critical, open, and informed. As represented in newspapers, however, such conversations were sociable, leisurely, and inconsequential, the way Joseph Addison and Richard Steele had described them in the *Spectator,* or else unified in clamorous applause, the way courtly writers described the voices of grateful subjects. There is a gap between our empirical histories of political development and eighteenth-century descriptions of the meaning of events. To understand that gap, it is necessary to consider metaphors and other figures as structures of significance. By identifying the figures writers used to imagine public discussion, this study attempts to explain how writers imagined more general interests, new modes of address, and enlarged arenas for discussion.

Chapter 1 traces the figuration of the coffeehouse back to the *Spectator* papers, which popularized the language of the coffeehouse public. The writers repeatedly described Mr. Spectator strolling from one coffeehouse to another, listening to conversations, and repeating them as emblematic of the state of the nation. These compelling images of talk moving from one comfortable space to another allowed the coffee house to become a metaphor for publicity comparable to the Roman Forum. The *Spectator*'s language became conventional in eighteenth-century British writing. Descriptions of coffeehouses as "schools of democracy," in which for a few pence a cobbler could share a newspaper and a political discussion with a peer of the realm, appear frequently in newspapers, books, and letters written in the eighteenth century.

The power of the image based on the familiar physical space of the coffee house came from the replication and circulation of businesses in an urban setting and of discourse in oral and printed media. The content of coffeehouse conversations, and the limited and exclusive nature of the social world at each coffeehouse, provided local, familiar, and specific images from which writers and readers could project a more general and abstract social world from the many simultaneous conversations taking place in coffeehouses in London (and Birmingham, Philadelphia, and Kingston). In the political conversations represented in the *Spectator* papers, conceptual languages of republican virtue and print modernity are employed to imagine the public sphere as an abstracted and replicated version of a familiar social space.

Chapter 2 examines the courtly public sphere produced and reproduced in the manuscript documents that surrounded the king's court and the levees of powerful men and women. Courtly writers consistently named this sphere "the public." It does not fit Habermas's definition of a critical public sphere, however, because it was not separate from the state. The court centered on the king and was the institution through which the executive arm of the government did its work. Through print, however, and through larger and larger circuits of communication, the eighteenth-century courtly sphere amplified its performances for a growing audience. Courtly writers consistently referred to the people they knew their words would reach as "the World." Print expanded this world of aristocratic families and patron-client obligations further than any network of gossip and manuscript transmission could do. Well after the middle of the eighteenth century, newspaper writers routinely described political events in terms of the "clamour" and "alarm" that could be heard in discussions among influential people, of "information" about the moods and inclinations of princes, and about who had been seen talking to whom and for how long. Although this audience for courtly news was a public in its size, its anonymity, and its abstraction, it was neither critical nor rational in Habermas's sense. Courtly writers, both in manuscript and in print, represented their own discourse as hierarchical, competitive, and factional.

Chapter 3 argues that the newspapers' representation of an anonymous group of readers engaged among themselves in exploring the importance of day-to-day political events is an effect of juxtapositions between figures of clamor and figures of coffeehouse chat. Commentary in eighteenth-century papers was often conveyed through "letters to the printer," written in some cases by a paper's staff; in others by advocates for particular individuals, groups, or policies; and in still others by apparently unaffiliated readers. The letters mobilized a bewildering array of literary devices, including dialogues, narratives, lectures, prophetic dreams, overheard coffeehouse conversations, observations of fictional visitors from Asia or Europe, and various combinations of the above. Over the course of the eighteenth century, these letters recorded the accretion of figures for political talk, as clamor was juxtaposed with coffeehouse talk, complaints, bon mots, and murmurs in the columns of the daily and weekly papers. Clamor provided letter writers with a figure for circulating, influential discourse. Juxtaposing figures based on clamor with figures based on coffeehouse chat, newspapers presented readers with a picture of public life located in a realm of self-referential, figurative, circulating talk. The talk itself was figured in familiar ways, but writers imagined an *arena* for talk more flexible, multiple, and critical than the courtly or sociable arenas from which its figures were drawn.

Chapter 4 examines newspaper reports that at first glance look less figurative than coffeehouse talk or clamor. Descriptions of parliamentary procedures and the activities of debating societies bear fewer markers of rhetorical complexity and figuration than the other representations examined earlier. But the differences between reports published before and after 1771 reveal their figurative nature. Changes in parliamentary reporting led to changes in reporting on all meetings. Before 1771, it was illegal to publish accounts of Parliament's deliberations. Newspaper writers attempted to avoid prosecution by employing pseudonyms, elaborate allegories, and circumlocutions. They evaluated the talk in Parliament in terms of honor and combat. In these forms Parliament served as a vehicle for figuration and for imagining circulating discourse. Debating societies modeled themselves upon it and gossips repeated their evaluations of the performances made in it. The quality of this figuration changed noticeably, however, after 1771 when the government stopped prosecuting printers for parliamentary reporting. As newspapers were freed from the necessity of elaborate circumlocution and reporters were able to take notes, articles on Parliament began including the details of procedure: agendas, motions, amendments, votes. These details framed and accompanied the more traditional accounts of towering eloquence and feeble pleading.

As newspaper writers began to use different language for reporting on Parliament's deliberations, they also began to use different language for describing the meetings of debating societies, charities, and civic associations. Like members of Parliament, participants in these groups could read newspaper accounts of their agendas, motions, and votes. A common term for describing their activities was "free and candid debate." Like coffeehouse talk or courtly clamor, free and candid debate was a figure for a complex and multilayered phenomenon. It referred to spaces around the city where such talk could take place: Parliament, the Robin Hood Society, the Society for the Encouragement of Arts and Manufactures. It also referred to the movement of talk from one place to another, as particular speeches, reports, or victories in debate were discussed and reported in other conversations and in print. And, finally, it referred to the relationship between any particular oral exchange and all the others known to be taking place in the "nation of politicians" British writers so frequently claimed to inhabit.

Changes in the level of detail and the content of political discussions as reported in the newspapers after 1771 suggest the power of the figuration at work in newspaper representations, even those that read like literal accounts. The conventions and content of conversations as they were reported in newspapers are related to concepts of circulation. Meetings can be described in detail, as matters of public interest, only when the space of the meeting and the details of the deliberations can be understood as available for replication and circulation. Candid debate, like coffeehouse talk and courtly clamor, is a figure of speech.

Debate itself, then, is not a necessary condition for political talk to be public, but rather one of several forms from which writers derived the concept of publicity. The necessary condition for a concept of public discourse is the process of figuring, of naming replication and circulation as familiar and comprehensible phenomena. The particular scenes of speech that served as vehicles for this metaphor varied in the eighteenth century from court and Parliament to coffeehouses, tea tables, and drawing rooms, a variety that suggests the possibility of imagining future publics based on other spaces and other groups.

The question of how a republican government derives legitimacy, of what makes an opinion or a discussion public, and of how actions by the state are understood and judged by citizens were vitally important to eighteenth-century writers. They continue to be so for us as we critically examine the origin stories that democratic government tells about itself in the context of debates about the possibility of open and fair discussion, of representing majorities and minorities, and of the connections between republican government and accessible print culture, capitalist development, and bourgeois sensibility. Following metaphors of communication from manuscript to print, or from conversation to manuscript, at a crucial moment in the history of republican thought reveals a process through which media, social scenes, and linguistic forms became tropes for imagining political ties to the strangers among whom national and public interest were shared.

1
Figuring Coffeehouse Talk in the *Spectator* and Its Heirs

> Being an idle man, I am a great lounger in Coffee-houses, and a constant reader of all News Papers. . . .
>
> *An Essay on the Style and Composition of Newspapers*, London, 1765

BY ASSOCIATING NEWSPAPERS WITH LOUNGING AND IDLENESS, THIS pamphlet's writer employed terms familiar to readers of midcentury periodical prose. The pamphlet, excerpted in the *London Chronicle* in October of 1765, presents an extensive satire upon newspapers and upon the society they represent. The writer skewers quack doctors, socially pretentious city merchants, misers, supporters of John Wilkes, and the newspaper writers who published their activities. Each element of the essay is conventional, from the opening reference to a coffeehouse lounger to the satiric picture of "the dress of a City lady bedizened out for the Assembly at Haberdashers-hall, where precedence is settled by the price of Madam's gown per yard." In employing such conventional references to contemporary society, eighteenth-century periodical writing revealed its dependence upon satire of its own qualities: novelty, emphemerality, quotidian detail, openness to new social groups.

Commentary on eighteenth-century periodicals has emphasized both this satire and their role in creating arenas for the development of rational critique, democratic access, and a bourgeois public sphere. The conflict between satirical regulation and liberated critique has been explored in discussions of Jürgen Habermas's claim that the papers participated in a rational and accessible public sphere. Recent scholars have explored these questions in examinations of the *Spectator* papers, from which the pamphleteer quoted above derived many of his terms and tropes. Work on the *Spectator* has centered on providing terms for understanding the papers' cultural project without assuming a telos focused on the development of a bourgeois public sphere, the American or French revolutions, or the eventual triumph of capitalism and mass media. Erin Mackie's reading of fashion, Scott Black's and Tedra O'Sell's analyses of narrative voice, and Brian Cowan's exploration of Whig politics all argue that the *Spectator*'s writers used contemporary culture to introduce and regulate novelty and innovation.[1]

According to these studies, the *Spectator* papers regulate critique, rather than liberating it. In this chapter, I use this concept of regulating critique to explain the *Spectator*'s influential representation of "talking politics." Like the "idle man" in the pamphlet, the *Spectator*'s citizens constantly chat in coffeehouses, thirst for news, watch over the constitution, and take positions on affairs of state. The papers imagine this talk, evaluate it, and provide their readers with concepts for making it comprehensible as a general social phenomenon. Those concepts for comprehending political talk are metaphors of circulation, tropes that figure the movement of speech, writing, and print around the city and the nation. In deploying these tropes, the *Spectator*'s writers borrowed republican language of virtue and disinterest, unmooring it from the specific constitutional claims of civic republicanism or the rational norms of the bourgeois public sphere. It was through the language developed in the papers and their inheritors that British newspaper writers articulated the concept of public opinion. Like urbanity and fashion, political talk concerned novelty and ephemera; the *Spectator* writers imagined and regulated it through figurative significations of circulating talk and print.

By looking closely at specific scenes of political conversation in the *Spectator* papers, we can see the way in which powerful concepts of republican virtue and print modernity are employed in the papers to imagine a public sphere as an abstracted and replicated version of a familiar social space. The "antifashion fashion" of political talk in the papers is the wise dispensing of opinions by a responsible, independent man among his friends; the dangerous and possibly tyrannical fashion is the "thirst for news" that makes men and women dependent upon courts and other distant scenes of political drama.[2] Talk and print, as media for communication, are both endowed with figurative significance as representations of political and social relations.

Spectator no. 452, written together by Joseph Addison and Alexander Pope, begins by claiming "there is no Humour in my Countrymen, which I am more enclined to wonder at, than their general Thirst after News." Comments on this "thirst" were already conventional in 1711, when the *Spectator* began publication.[3] By describing the propensity to participate in political discourse as a physical appetite, the writers linked it with taste, luxury, and consumption. This "general thirst" can be discussed in the same terms as the general desire for jeweled snuff-boxes or raree-shows discussed so extensively in the *Spectator* papers. The passage goes on to ridicule this thirst: "Our Time lies heavy on our Hands till the Arrival of a fresh Mail: We long to receive further Particulars, to hear what will be the next Step, or what will be the Consequences of that which has been already taken. A Westerly Wind keeps the whole Town in Suspence, and puts a stop to Conversation" (iv: 90). In her study of fashion in the *Spectator,* Erin Mackie has pointed out how frequently the language of tyranny is used to describe social trends; people are forced to wear particular clothes, speak in particular ways, and enjoy particular amusements because they are fashionable.[4] In the same way, this passage describes the town as enslaved to the news through a desire for novelty (a fresh mail) and detail (further particulars). When a westerly wind keeps ships out of the Channel and stops the circulation of letters from the continent, London is silenced. The papers frequently lampoon people whose minds are empty or blank until they run across some novelty with which to fill them for the day; the thirst for news, this passage suggests, makes the whole city either blank or enslaved to novelty.

It is interesting to juxtapose this passage with Jürgen Habermas's account of the place of news in European history:

> The traffic in news . . . developed alongside the traffic in commodities. . . . With the expansion of trade, merchants' market-oriented calculations required more frequent and more exact information about distant events. . . . The merchants organized the first mail routes, the so-called ordinary mail, departing on assigned days. The great trade cities became at the same time centers for the traffic in news; the organization of this traffic on a *continuous* basis became imperative to the degree to which the exchange of commodities and of securities became continuous.[5]

It was this structure of continuously circulating information exchange, Habermas argues, that founded the periodical press. In criticizing the thirst for news, the *Spectator* writers were criticizing the social and economic institutions that made their own publication possible. The *Spectator* writers do not invoke calculation or the imperatives of trade in their account of the news, however. They describe the news as a luxury item for jaded consumers rather than material for rational calculation.

Erin Mackie's reading of the papers' simultaneous staging and regulation of fashion can help us understand this paradoxical participation in and condemnation of the thirst for news. She explains why fashion is a helpful category of analysis: "defined by novelty, acceleration, and apparently arbitrary and thus unpredictable outcomes, fashion, perceived as a certain kind of (usually faulty) criterion of selection, serves as a magnet for criticism of the play of these forces in cultural, economic, political, and social life."[6] The *Spectator* papers, she argues, attempt to regulate their readers' tastes, while denying "their own fashionability as modish lifestyle magazines. In them we find the logic of antifashion fashion: what is really stylistically desirable is defined against what is merely 'fashionable.'"[7] Defined in Mackie's terms, news is also a fashion. The thirst for news causes Londoners, according to the *Spectator,* to wait for the foreign mail, which brings "novelty, acceleration, and apparently arbitrary and thus unpredictable outcomes." Distant battles, the births and deaths of princes, and the ins and outs of court favorites and ministers all exercised a tyranny similar to the trend in hoop petticoats. The *Spectator* papers commodified metaphors of circulation, inviting consumers to purchase constantly renewed essays in which the desire for political novelty was adjusted, diverted, and further circulated. Political discourse, like fashion and opera, was treated as an object of cultural criticism, and thus its regulation was itself commodified.

The *Spectator* has taken an important place in accounts of the development of the bourgeois public sphere, a central element of which, as Habermas points out in the passage above, is the *continuous* circulation of discourse. Rather than isolated, authoritative edicts produced by church or state, the public sphere is constituted by accessible, ongoing discourse. Michael Warner and Adrian Johns have explained how print technology symbolically represented that continuous circulation, as well as providing the physical machinery to make it possible. The *Spectator* papers' periodical appearance, frequent inclusion of letters from readers, and anonymous "representative" figures have all been seen as formal devices for making such continuous, accessible discourse a central part of eighteenth-century culture.[8]

Habermas and Warner, reading this understanding of print's technological and symbolic capacities together with J. G. A. Pocock's concept of a modernized version of civic republicanism, have given the *Spectator* a role in liberating political discourse from the domination of church and state.[9] Brian Cowan has revised this view by pointing out that "much of the success of the *Spectator* project" derived from the writers' ability "to shift the discussion away from the contentious issues of religious politics [and] . . . controversial constitutional principles. . . . In the long run, [the papers] provided the foundations for a view of Whiggery as moderate, progressive, and polite."[10] Cowan's work makes it impossible to argue any longer that the *Spectator* is part of a political project directed toward restoring a robust public sphere modeled on Roman civic republicanism or the debates that preceded the Civil War, or even toward the version of Whig ideas that the rebellious American colonists would articulate later in the century.

Republican ideas, however, do play an important part in the imaginative project of the *Spectator* papers, and jettisoning these concepts entirely would make it difficult to explain the papers' influential contribution to British periodical writing on politics. Warner's link between periodicity and the metaphorical power of print can help us make the connection between the *Spectator* and political writing later in the century. It is the *Spectator* writers' ability to represent and create metaphors from the media of the papers' circulation that proved to be so influential. Unlike their predecessors, the papers yoked familiar gibes against gossip and newsmongering to a series of images of language moving through an anonymous, polite, tasteful, and moral readership. The papers successfully staked a claim to be both periodical and moral, to contain political chatter while speaking to and for a general public. Readings of the papers' anxieties about faction, commodification, and newsmongering show how difficult a claim this was to stake. According to Warner, print, with its assurance of anonymity, was a modern way of invoking the "republican norm of disinterest."[11] By appearing in print rather than in manuscript, texts claimed to be virtuous in republican terms, rather than connected to individuals and their interests and desires. This is a figurative quality rather than an inherent aspect of the products of printing presses. The machines that produced printed pages and the pages themselves represented disinterest and anonymity to a culture engaged in defining its relation to global markets, merchantile capitalism, and other abstract social phenomena.

Using this idea that a medium such as print can endow a text with figurative power, I argue that the papers' versatility and influence for later political periodical writers were produced by figures of talk and print. The *Spectator* writers put figures based on these two media in productive relation to each other, imagining a world of discourse both accessible and regulated, diverting and virtuous. Later writers exploited these figures to serve political ends beyond the specific exigencies of Anne's reign: the paper's strategies served both Tory opposition and American republicanism later in the century.[12] For the *Spectator* writers and for their heirs, these figures enabled an imagined polity of polite discussion haunted by the specter of courtly gossip and idle lounging.

Cowan argues that the specific political occasion for the *Spectator*'s first issues was a Whig attempt to divert public interest from the dramatic events of the Sacheverell trial. Such diversion requires periodicity—the papers provided something novel three times a week. Scott Black makes a related argument at the level of the papers' narrative style: "such 'occasional papers' comment on the 'Irregularities' (4:27) of the day by matching its vagaries with a literary form organized precisely by such irregularity. This new form redeems the occasional, mimicking its irregularities, and validates the experience of the mundane world, offering it as worthy of being noted, represented, and understood."[13] To divert their readers from high political drama, the papers infuse the mundane irregularities of everyday life with importance and attention. The novelty and detail Mackie associates with fashion are here presented in the context of the day-by-day experiences of contemporary life. The language of disinterest derived from republican thought is used to ennoble the image of readers ignoring divisive political events and focusing on a new play or the interactions happening over their own tea tables. The papers address their readers as separate from an ongoing participation in oral and print discourse about the actions of the state. But they provide a substitute that is also circulating, replicated, novel, diverting, and periodical.

Figurative language centered on particular scenes of political talk enabled the *Spectator*'s writers to create this substitution. For example, in no. 43 Steele describes people interested in political news as "Persons, who for the want of something to do, out of a certain Vacancy of Thought, rather than Curiosity, are ever meddling with things for which they are unfit."[14] This distinction between "vacancy of thought" and "curiosity" is like the distinction between "taste" and "fashion." In each pair, the two terms are functionally the same, causing people to search out novelty and detail, but they are different in their relation to a firm standard of value, such as intelligence or natural beauty. In this essay, Steele ridicules a club of Oxford dons. He writes a satirical letter purporting to be from "Abraham Froth," a member of the club. The purpose of the club, according to Froth, is "to settle the Nation at home, and to carry on the War abroad, where and in what manner we see fit:

If other People are not of our Opinion, we can't help that." Such a dismissal of others' opinions suggests that the outcome of such conversations is always either conflict or irrelevance.

Abraham Froth describes the opinions of his group:

> We are much offended at the Act for Importing French Wines. . . . We look upon a certain Northern Prince's march, in Conjunction with Infidels, to be palpably against our good Will and Liking, and . . . a most dangerous Innovation; and we are by no means yet sure, that some People are not at the bottom on't. . . . We think we have at last done the Business with the Malecontents in Hungary, and shall clap up a Peace there. What the Neutrality Army is to do, or what the Army in Flanders, and what two or three other Princes, is not yet fully determined among us. . . .

This passage parodies the self-important tone of someone proud of receiving a constant supply of news. His insinuation that "some People" might be behind the alliance between Charles XII of Sweden and the grand signior suggests that he has information so fresh and important that he cannot divulge in his letter. The hearty informality with which he writes of "clapping up a Peace," and "two or three other Princes" reveals his overconfidence in deciding the affairs of the world from behind a tankard in Oxford. This entire conversation is conducted in the language of dependency. In deciding the affairs of armies and princes, the club is dependent for its conversation on events happening at courts and on distant battlefields. The members pass their time by interpreting that information and basing predictions upon their interpretations, thus displaying appetites for detail and novelty that the *Spectator* papers consistently associate with ridiculous fashions in other commodities.

What is the standard of value that would make an interest in the news a good thing, "curiosity" rather than a dangerous "vacancy of thought"? Pocock's analysis of leisure and virtue in republican thought can help to answer that question:

> the Englishman had begun to envisage himself [by the seventeenth century] as civic individual through the use of Aristotelian and civic humanist categories, which required among other things that there be a material foundation, the equivalent of Aristotle's *oikos*, for his independence, leisure and virtue. The nature of this equivalent had been described for him, first by Machiavelli in terms of arms, second by Harrington in terms of property; and the realities of the seventeenth-century social structure had established as paradigmatic the image of the freeholder, founded upon real or landed property

> which was inheritable rather than marketable, was protected by the ancient sanctions of the common law, and brought with it membership in the related structures of the militia and the parliamentary electorate, thus guaranteeing civic virtue.[15]

The members of Froth's club enjoy leisure, but they do not use that leisure in ways that shore up their independence and virtue. Just as a taste for luxury could cause a British freeholder to give up his landed property for the fickle whims of credit and speculation, a taste for news could cause him to give up independent opinions for the dependence upon a "fresh mail"—or a newspaper.

Two different media are represented in the passage describing Froth's club, and each carries figurative significance. Print serves as a metaphor for disinterest, as Warner argues. The *Spectator* papers themselves deliver satire within a framework of anonymity and ironic distance. But political talk is more suspect. Abraham Froth is as much a representative figure as Mr. Spectator. His club is one of the many the paper represents to its readers as familiar elements of the urban landscape. Clubs, coffeehouses, and tea tables are used to imagine political talk as an avenue for the corruption inherent in a thirst for news. In the introduction to this study, we saw that Horace Walpole used different media empirically and figuratively. Here, the *Spectator's* writers do the same, distinguishing between media as they create metaphorical figures of circulating discourse. Literally using print as a medium for reaching their readers, the writers use talk metaphorically to imaginatively comprehend that act of communication.

Jürgen Habermas's description of the place of coffeehouses and clubs in the bourgeois public sphere does not distinguish between oral and printed media, or between the empirical existence and the figurative significance of any medium: "Just as Dryden, surrounded by the new generation of writers, joined the battle of the 'ancients and moderns' at Will's, Addison and Steele a little later convened their 'little senate' at Button's; so too in the Rotary Club, presided over by Milton's secretary, Marvell and Pepys met with Harrington who here probably presented the republican ideas of his *Oceana*. . . . Thus critical debate ignited by works of literature and art was soon extended to include economic and political disputes."[16] Habermas fits the *Spectator* writers' own club into a narrative in which literary criticism paves the way for political criticism, although he pulls Milton, Marvell, and Pepys out of chronological order to do so. Arguing along similar lines, Steve Pincus claims that by the late seventeenth century, coffeehouses were a central institution of English life because "the center of English political discourse had shifted in favor of an optimistic view of human rationality." Charles II's attempt to shut down coffeehouses had to be withdrawn after less than two weeks because "the idea of the public sphere had clearly been embraced by the English political nation."[17]

Both Habermas and Pincus connect oral and printed discourse, and the representation of that discourse in figures such as coffeehouse talk, with rational standards of judgment and with political consequences that can be labeled, broadly, republican. Can Abraham Froth's letter be seen as a fictionalized version of such coffeehouse talk? I argue that there is an important distinction between the actual club meetings of Addison and Steele and the fictional but representative club meetings that fill the pages of the papers. As Tedra O'Sell has argued, "the role of the essay periodical as text [is] central to an understanding of the larger fiction of the public sphere, a fiction built out of texts."[18] Abraham Froth, with his personified name, is a representative figure. He invites readers to recognize his way of writing in other texts and conversations and to imagine his club as one of many meeting in many spaces around the city and nation. And, crucially, this picture of a political club is negative. "Critical debate" is not "ignited" here but rather questions are "settled," and air is filled not with fire but with froth. In this way, periodical essays endow political talk with powerful figurative significance as a general, widespread, accessible activity, while regulating the dangerous elements of conflict and desire associated with it.

The *Spectator* papers often locate the conflicts and desires of politics at court. Rather than imagining political talk as critical of the actions of the state, the papers imagine it as oriented by and deriving from the monarchal center of the nation. In no. 193, published October 11, 1711, Steele describes the people who frequent the Drawing Room and "the Levees of Great Men" in the same language of tyranny and appetite we saw above:

> Those whom we call good Courtiers . . . are got into a habit of being Servile with an Air, and enjoy a certain Vanity in being known for understanding how the World passes. In the pleasure of this they can rise early, go abroad sleek and well dressed, with no other Hope or Purpose but to make a Bow to a Man in Court Favour, and be thought, by some insignificant smile of his, not a little engaged in his Interests and Fortunes. It is wondrous that a Man can get over the Natural Existence and Possession of his own Mind so

> far, as to take delight either in paying or receiving such cold and repeated Civilities. (2:257)

The "Applications and Addresses" made at court are all, in Steele's version, "vain." Nothing can really be gained or accomplished, at least nothing so valuable as to be worth the time and servility required. Courtiers have "no Hope or Purpose" and their lives are unnatural, dispossessed, and cold. This language derives from the republican terms analyzed by Pocock: nature and possession, the guarantees of independence, have been given up in favor of fickle and speculative values founded in other people's ideas—being "thought" by others to be engaged in the great man's interests is this courtier's whole goal. Steele uses images of theft and value to suggest the corruption intrinsic to court talk, the same kind of corruption practiced by kings who give pensions in order to ensure votes in Parliament. As in the earlier passage about the thirst for news, the terms Mackie identifies with fashion and antifashion are here used to characterize valueless political talk. Not only is the courtier "sleek and well dressed," his "vanity" derives from court conversations that, like the *Spectator* itself, are periodical: "repeated civilities." Novelty, detail, and repetition, the signs of all cultural practices and objects the papers attempt to regulate, are located in the case of politics at the court. In using such terms, the *Spectator* writers separate their own medium, print, from the dangerous tendencies associated with talk. Although both print and talk are periodical and circulating, talk is the more potentially corrupt.

When the *Spectator* papers represent talk, and especially political talk, circulation itself is often associated with dependency. Coining the term "quidnunc" in the *Tatler*, the *Spectator*'s predecessor, Steele had characterized a person who always asks "what now?" This question reveals a dependency upon novelty and detail. In a letter from "Tho. Quid-nunc" published in no. 625, all the media for circulating discourse are presented as endangered by contaminating political talk. Each medium is figured as the center of a social institution that must be named and regulated. Gossip, manuscript letters, and the *Spectator* itself feature in this satirical vision of the dangers of news. Quid-nunc tells Mr. Spectator:

> I wonder that, in the present Situation of Affairs, you can take Pleasure in writing any thing but News; for, in a Word, who minds any thing else? The Pleasure of increasing in Knowledge, and learning something new every Hour of Life, is the noblest Entertainment of a Rational Creature. I have a

very good Ear for a Secret, and am naturally of a communicative Temper, by which means I am capable of doing you great Services in this way. In order to make my self useful, I am early in the Antichamber, where I thrust my Head into the thick of the Press, and catch the News, at the opening of the Door, while it is warm. Sometimes I stand by the Beef-Eaters, and take the Buz as it passes by me. At other times I lay my Ear close to the Wall, and suck in many a valuable Whisper, as it runs in a straight Line from Corner to Corner. When I am weary with standing, I repair to one of the neighboring Coffee-houses, where I sit sometimes for a whole Day, and have the News, as it comes from Court, fresh and fresh. In short Sir, I spare no pains to know how the World goes. A Piece of News loses its Flavour when it hath been Hour in the Air. I love, if I may so speak, to have it fresh from the Tree; and to convey it to my Friends before it is faded. Accordingly my Expences in Coach-hire make no small Article; which you may believe, when I assure you, that I post away from Coffee-house to Coffee-house, and forestall the *Evening-Post* by two Hours. There is a certain Gentleman, who hath given me the slip twice or thrice, and hath been before-hand with me at *Child's*. But I have played him a Trick. I have purchased a Pair of the best Coach-horses I could buy for Money, and now let him out-strip me if he can. Once more, Mr. SPECTATOR, let me advise you to deal in News. You may depend upon my Assistance. But I must break off abruptly, for I have twenty Letters to write.

Yours, in haste, Tho. Quid-nunc (5:136).

Movement itself is associated with expense, here, and thus with the dangers of luxury. Quid-nunc's appetites are indicated by the way he thrusts his head into the crowd and sucks news into his ear. The warm, fresh fruit from the tree of news suggests the knowledge of good and evil that Quid-nunc is not morally equipped to handle. News itself is seen as coming only from the court, where Beefeaters guard the antechamber in which the king may be seen conversing with his favored friends and dependents. Coffeehouses, rather than institutions separate from the court, are here seen as extensions of it, where both talk and newspapers replicate the "Buz" that runs from corner to corner in that emblematic space.

Interestingly, Donald Bond notes in his edition of the *Spectator* papers that the reference to the "*Evening-Post*" is probably not to the newspaper of that name but to the evening mail. The drinkers at coffeehouses received letters that had been posted just before the post-houses closed at 9 p.m., often letters relating what had happened at court that morning. This is a reminder that like print and talk, manuscript also circulated around the city, providing novelty and extending the range of courtly dependency. Talk and letters are both vehicles for figures that represent a world of noisy, idle dependency, fueled by a desire for novelty and fed by court gossip.

The *Spectator* papers do propose an alternative to news as a corrupting luxury. In the same way that, according to Mackie, "what is really stylistically desirable is defined against what is merely 'fashionable,'" a form of political talk associated with judgment is contrasted to the vapid exchange of novelties.[19] Even in these ideals of tasteful and independent political discourse, however, the specter of courts and the thirst for news is always lurking. In no. 49, Steele describes coffee houses as little courts, which can be virtuous or corrupt according to the temperament of the men who dominate them:

> We are very Curious to observe the Behaviour of Great Men and their Clients; but the same Passions and Interests move Men in lower Spheres; and I (that have nothing else to do, but make Observations) see in every Parish, Street, Lane, and Alley of this Populous City, a little Potentate that has his Court, and his Flatterers who lay Snares for his Affection and Favour, by the same Arts that are practiced upon Men in higher Stations. In the Place I most usually frequent, Men differ rather in the time of Day in which they make a Figure, than in any real Greatness above one another. . . . Eubulus presides over the middle Hours of the Day, when this Assembly of Men meet together. He enjoys a great Fortune handsomely, without launching into Expense, and exerts many noble and useful Qualities, without appearing in any publick Employment. . . .
>
> Eubulus has so great an Authority in his little Diurnal Audience, that when he shakes his Head at any Piece of publick News, they all of them appear dejected; and, on the contrary, go home to their Dinners with a good Stomach and cheerful Aspect, when Eubulus seems to intimate that Things go well. Nay, their Veneration towards him is so great, that when they are in other Company they speak and act after him; are Wise in his Sentences, are no sooner sat down at their own Tables, but they hope or fear, rejoice or despond as they saw him do at the Coffee-house. In a word, every Man is Eubulus as soon as his Back is turn'd. (1: 209–11).

Like the Athenian statesman described by Xenophon as a fiscal genius, this independent and prosperous man cares for wealth not by active engagement in commerce but by his ability to keep the news from dominating him. Here, too, circulation is the central characteristic of talk and of news. But Eubulus is able to apply wise judgment, unlike a

Quid-nunc who prizes the news simply for its newness. Because he does not appear in any "public employment" or "launch" his fortune into dangerous ventures, he has access to the source of value mentioned by Pocock—the independence of inherited wealth, the "material foundation . . . for leisure and virtue." Although the *Spectator* frequently argues in favor of commerce, in this case Eubulus's money is connected to the respect he receives from his associates and the way he handles news without becoming a slave to novelty.[20] Thus he is one of the men always "at home, and in quiet Possession of the present Instant, as it passes, without desiring to Quicken it by gratifying any Passion, or prosecuting any new Design" (1:210). This material, political, and spiritual independence enable Eubulus to participate in the circulation of news as it ought to be. In this passage, political talk partakes of the qualities associated with print: distance from particular hands, bodies, and interests. It is also explicitly gendered male, unlike much of the "philosophy" presented in the papers, which Mr. Spectator often claims is directed at female tea tables as well as male coffeehouses. This line of tension points to the fictiveness of the figurative link the papers make between particular spaces and a general readership.

By representing such interactions, the *Spectator* papers make the image of an intimate club figurative. That figure organizes and familiarizes the papers' role as circulating printed objects. A general, anonymous, public audience such as that reached by the papers is comprehensible not through projecting a single boundary that would enclose everyone together. An "imagined community," "public sphere," or "forum" is not suggested by these images.[21] Instead, a national group is imagined through the juxtaposition of smaller groups—"worlds" of action, tables in a coffeehouse, coffeehouses in a city—and the circulation of discourse among them. An abstraction, which we could call society, readership, or public, is built from figures of more limited and thus visualizable communities, connected to each other by circulating print and to virtue by the language of disinterest. In an often-quoted passage, Addison describes Mr. Spectator's movement from one club or assembly to another:

> I have passed my latter Years in this City, where I am frequently seen in most publick Places, tho' there are not above half a dozen of my select Friends that know me; of whom my next Paper shall give a more particular Account. There is no Place of general Resort, wherein I do not often make my Appearance; sometimes I am seen thrusting my Head into a Round of

> Politicians at *Will's*, and listning with great Attention to the Narratives that are made in those little Circular Audiences. Sometimes I smoak a Pipe at *Child's*; and whilst I seem attentive to nothing but the *Post-Man*, overhear the Conversation of every Table in the Room. I appear on *Sunday* Nights at St. *James's* Coffee-House, and sometimes join the little Committee of Politicks in the Inner-Room, as one who comes there to hear and improve. My Face is likewise very well known at the *Grecian*, the *Cocoa-Tree*, and in the Theaters both of *Drury-Lane*, and the *Hay-Market*. I have been taken for a Merchant upon the Exchange for above these ten Years, and sometimes pass for a *Jew* in the Assembly of Stock-Jobbers at *Jonathan's*. In short, where-ever I see a Cluster of People I always mix with them, tho' I never open my Lips but in my own Club. (1:4)

The concluding sentence of this paragraph represents discourse circulating among multiple replicated spaces. The social vision Addison presents here is made up of "clusters" of talking people. Mr. Spectator's particular importance is that he listens to the talk in these various venues and speaks only "in my own club," into which the readers of the paper are invited through the replicated and circulated copies of the *Spectator* papers themselves. Like Eubulus, Mr. Spectator derives his authority from his relationship to those who value his ideas because he has exercised judgment upon the news he has heard, mediating and distancing it from particular political interests.

The spaces named in the passage above are called both "publick" and "general." Both words indicate openness, accessibility, and familiarity, and treat those qualities as already understood by readers. The familiar tone in which "those little circular audiences" at Will's, or "the little committee of politics in the Inner-Room" at the St. James's are mentioned, as if already known to the reader, indicates a shared knowledge of the city and its spaces. The familiarity and intimacy of these spaces, created for readers by the papers' familiar address, provides a helpful and concrete physical image for understanding the city and the nation as constituted through circulating discourse. By infusing talk with the abstraction and distance associated with print, these images of multiplied spaces regulate the dangers of courtly intrigue and idle novelty inherent in political talk.

The *Spectator* papers negotiate these abstractions not by imagining a single, central coffee house where politics and art and business and theater are all discussed by men and women of all sorts and degrees, but by an image of circulation and replication. Smoking a pipe at Child's coffeehouse and pretending to read the paper, Mr. Spectator can "overhear the Conversation of every Table in the Room." In this single image, Addison creates great figurative significance for the circulation of discourse among replicated spaces. Each table is having its own conversation, but that conversation is available to listeners at other tables, especially to a silent, critical man like Mr. Spectator. Conversation is general or public not because it is addressed directly to a large, anonymous group, but because it is available for circulation among smaller, local groups. Circulation is an abstract concept, like society, but it is easy to visualize in the context of a single wanderer and listener among tables in a large room.

The images of people and talk circulating among these spaces suggest that the spaces are replicated versions of each other. Child's may be one of a kind, but the paper also addresses generalized "coffee houses and tea tables" among which an opinion on the latest play or a bon mot circulates. By representing this movement of discourse among and around replicated spaces, the writers found a way to formulate the phenomenon that recent scholars have named "print culture." By listening to "every table in the room" and then retelling what he has heard to his own clubmates, Mr. Spectator does on a small scale what a newspaper printer does on a larger scale: collect information, reproduce it, and circulate it. By imagining such circulation as an abstracted version of the wise counsel shared by a good man with his intimate friends, the writers suggest that readers see circulation as a general social phenomenon inoculated from the dangerous propensities of a thirst for news. Using figures of talk and print to signify circulating discourse in general, the *Spectator* papers present an abstracted sense of the talk of the town that is at the same time free and regulated, desirable and virtuous, fashionable and disinterested.

Other contemporary writers also used images of conversational spaces and replicated copies to describe the importance of the *Spectator* papers. John Gay, in a 1711 pamphlet *The Present State of Wit,* comments that the *Spectator* was "in every ones Hand, and a constant Topick for our Morning Conversation at Tea-Tables, and Coffee-houses." Multiple copies, multiple hands, and multiple intimate, familiar spaces help to figure the social significance of the paper's readership. Hugh Blair uses the same image of copies in multiple hands in his influential *Essays Moral and Literary:* "The *Spectator* . . . is a book which is in the hands of every one, and which cannot be praised too highly. The good sense, the good writing, the useful morality, and the admirable vein of humor which abound in it, render it one of those standard books which have done the greatest honor to the English nation."[22] The paper is important and authoritative through replication, both in print and in speech. It is in every hand and in every conversation. Its readers are not Quidnuncs, however, because their discourse circulates among little assemblies figured as clubs of the virtuous and independent men who determine what is "standard" and "useful," rather than among courts of dependent newsmongers.

As part of this project, London itself becomes a vehicle for figurations of circulating discourse. *Spectator* no. 3 begins "in one of my late Rambles, or rather Speculations, I looked into the great Hall where the Bank is kept. . . ." This image introduces an elaborate allegory about public credit. Credit, like fashion and news, presented both dangers and possibilities for the Whig party, for periodical essayists, and for Mr. Spectator. All were being reimagined as more free-ranging, more accessible, and more abstract. By renaming "rambles" as "speculations," Addison indicates the figurative importance of Mr. Spectator's wanderings. When he walks, Mr. Spectator speculates. The word connotes both philosophical and financial exploration. As an intellectual activity, speculating is trying out an idea, positing. As a financial one, it is taking a risk, investing in the hope of exploiting a market that may or may not exist. Such a word is a fitting introduction for an allegory supporting free trade. But it is also a fitting name for the relation between the rambles represented in the paper and the activity into which the paper invites its readers. Representations of Mr. Spectator's walks were written down in manuscript, printed on multiple similar pieces of paper, and transported around the city and the empire to multiple readers. In this way, the paper was a commodity, a speculation on the part of its writers and printers that a multiplicity of buyers existed. But Mr. Spectator's rambles were also aimless, disinterested, and anonymous, thus distancing his ideas from the taint of personal ambition, stockjobbing, and corruption. His rambles gave him the opportunity to judge, evaluate, and compare the conversations he heard in different spaces, and thus to distill them further away from the oral figures of court hangers-on and idle coffeehouse loungers and toward the figures of disinterested, distanced, print. A reader of the *Spectator* papers is invited not to literally overhear what has been said at Child's but to hold in his or her hands a distillation of that talk, created through a speculative ramble from one table to another and from one coffeehouse to another.

By equating rambling with speculation, this passage points out the figurative nature of all its other descriptions of Mr. Spectator's movement between one space and another. Rather than an empirical description of the city's places of public resort, the paper presents a metaphorical figure for conveying the significance of a particular kind of conversation. A nested series of images, each one step more abstract than the last, attributes the significance of each conversation to a larger social world surrounding it. At a particular coffeehouse, Mr. Spectator can overhear the conversation "at every table." On a larger scale, Mr. Spectator can go from one coffeehouse to another. On a larger scale than that, he can write down what he has heard, have it printed on thousands of identical sheets of paper, and send them around the city, the country, and the empire.

The *Spectator*'s images of rambling and chatting abstract the concepts of replication and circulation in order to represent periodical publishing as both virtuous and diverting. The *Spectator* uses the coffeehouse space, in the passages quoted above and in many more that followed, as a visual image of the group into which readers are invited by gestures like the off-hand reference to the "inner-room" at a particular house. When Mr. Spectator claims that "I never open my lips but in my own Club," he includes his readers in that club and makes the paper itself one of the replicated spaces in which discourse circulating around the city is available to a particular small group.

The power of the paper's capacity to represent urban life as a subject of self-conscious and self-reflexive contemplation through images of coffeehouse talk can be seen in the way James Boswell uses the same images in his journal. A particularly receptive consumer of figures for self-consciousness, Boswell calls upon the *Spectator*'s images in precisely the terms suggested by the early issues of the journal. He records a political dialogue he has participated in at Child's coffee house, noting that "the *Spectator* mentions his being seen at Child's, which makes me have an affection for it. I think myself like him, and am serenely happy there."[23] The conversation is not particularly edifying, although Boswell is happy with a metaphor he used. Its importance is not in precisely what was said, but in having that kind of conversation in that kind of place, replicating what one has read.

The participants in the public life described by the *Spectator* are participants specifically because they are part of a continuous, accessible, and mediated conversation. Eloquence, or any attempt to "make a figure" or stand out from a group, is either ignored or criticized by the writers. It is in conversation among themselves that people become part of that abstracted entity, the public, as defined through Mr. Spectator's rambles or speculations. Unlike a single forum or sphere addressed by an orator, the coffeehouse serves as a figure for a series of spaces in which multiple conversations take place.

Writers later in the century relied upon the *Spectator*'s figures of circulating discourse and refined judgment, as well as its suspicion of the dangerous tendencies of a thirst for news. By the 1760s, political essayists were still referring familiarly to coffeehouse talk in periodical writing. As they did so, however, they often found themselves ridiculing political conversation itself for its dependence on novelty and its fashionable uselessness. The *Public Advertiser* of November 16, 1770 contained two letters that began by calling up the social world represented in the *Spectator*. "Panurge" begins his letter by explaining, "after I had just eaten my Mutton Chop Yesterday in the public Room at Appleby's, I heard a monstrous Noise and scuffling above stairs. . . ." He uses this to introduce a satire on John Wilkes, who has, he says, been fistfighting in an upper room. Another letter writer begins, "As your paper, Mr. Woodfall, is constantly brought to me with my Dish of Coffee and Muffin, I have just had the Pleasure of seeing and perusing the Letter that Mr. Wilkes has favoured you and the public with. . . ." The association between particular spaces and the capacity of political talk to circulate, in such passages, constitutes public opinion as a figure difficult to imagine without links to particular spaces, dishes of coffee, or muffins. In each of these cases, the disreputable nature of the space and the activities engaged in there also characterize the political position the writer will criticize.

Writing to the *London Evening Post* earlier the same year, "Cato" argued against favoritism in the current administration by claiming that "there is not a man about *St. James's*, or *Richmond*, who does not *know*—There is not a Merchant or principal Tradesman in town—there is not a man to be met with in the street—- who does not *believe* that the Favourite is still behind the curtain, and in full possession of his pernicious, and I will venture to call it, for some people, *fatal influence*."[24] By naming the specific places where men with particular sorts of knowledge are to be met and by claiming that knowledge is to be gained by thinking about the men met in the street, this writer uses a figure similar to Mr. Spectator's rambles from table to table and from coffeehouse to coffeehouse. Like the coffee and muffin or the noises upstairs, the specific spaces in this passage allow the writers to abstract the concepts of circulating discourse, continuous discussion, and the dangers and productive possibilities of a thirst for news.

As conventions for representing circulating discussions of topics of general interest, such figures served political writers well. For making claims in favor of particular policies, strategies, or parties, however, they created difficulties. As developed in the *Spectator,* these concepts imply that sociability and circulation are threatened by conflict, self-importance, and idleness. Writers using these figures thus continued to dismiss and disparage political talk even as they made political arguments. The productive but limiting nature of these figures can be seen in a poem published in the *London Chronicle* for October 17, 1765:

The Moralist

I.

Was it not for small talk, and nonsensical flight,
  Half the world would not know what to say;
Nay, STEVENS his *Lectures on Heads* would not write,
  Or FOOTE hardly know what to play.

II.

The wise men dispers'd, in confusion all seem,
  With ploddings and jostlings of State,
That mimick and satire have stol'n into esteem,
  And become ev'n Tea-table chat.

III.

As winter draws nigh, and the Dramas begin,
  Let us something material pursue;
Let the great folk agree, and the worthy come in,
  And let GARRICK old SHAKESPEARE renew.

IV.

Let writers on party drop stupid offence,
  Who have talents may otherwise show 'em;
While nonsense and squawling rule music and sense,
  Men of parts think the taste much below 'em.

V.

Since Thro the Wood Laddie, Let her go, let her go,
  Is the pitch of this tweedledum crisis;
How can Stanley, Boyce, Baildon, and Nares undergo,
  To—grind razors[25]—their taste each so nice is?

VI.

Let ingenious inditers once more take the pen,
And lash with true morals, not railings;
Then composers will shine and bright wisdom again
Will direct how to mend our late failings.

VII.

Let coffee-house talk be no longer low chatt'rings,
Or intentional arguments raise,
Or politics e'er be attended with flatt'rings,
Or no statesman have more than due praise.

VIII.

Let honor, truth, honesty, aboveboard appear,
As the standard of Old England's glory;
Of Wills o' Bagshot or Twitchers, let each place be clear.
Nor define more on Scot, Whig, or Tory.

JO. AN DRIWS

This poem provides an example of the extent to which the figures for circulating discourse found in the *Spectator* had become conventional in newspaper writing. Like the *Spectator* writers, this writer assumes that the virtue of the town can be evaluated in terms of the good taste of its entertainments and that both are based in uncorrupted politics. The poem equates the degeneration of political discourse with a debased theatrical scene and treats both together as the source of "small talk," "tea-table chat," and "coffee-house talk." In the renewed and glorious England the speaker calls for, political writers would "lash with true morals, not railings" at the same time that Garrick renews "old Shakespeare." Opera composers such William Boyce, John Stanley, Howard Baildon, and James Nares would be able to separate themselves from the crisis in political affairs and thus from the low music performed at Sadler's Wells. The conversations held by ordinary people, "half the world," around their coffee and tea cups are part of a large and interconnected whole with philosophical writing, theater, opera, political writing, poetry, and the politics taking place between and among administrations. The way English men and women talk in particular spaces, the performances of actors, and the writing of political essayists are all treated as specific cases of a more general phenomenon: what the world says.

In borrowing these figures from the *Spectator,* the writer also borrows a suspicion of conflict and of party. The last lines of the poem ask for an end to attacks on individuals (like the Earl of Sandwich, who was often lampooned as "Jemmy Twitcher"). The final line of the poem calls for honor, truth, and honesty to replace discussions of Whig and Tory and the Earl of Bute's Scottishness. These last lines indicate the confining nature of such figures for writers desiring to argue in favor of any political particulars: individuals, strategies, or policies. While honor, truth, and honesty are undeniably desirable qualities, they are so very abstract that other qualities must be added to them to make determinations on questions of, for instance, internal and external taxation or the value of a particular clause in a peace treaty. For the talk of the town to be virtuous and tasteful, this writer suggests, it must turn away from the "ploddings and jostlings of state" and toward a renewed and purified cultural scene that is both dependent upon and dismissive of the thirst for political news. The *Spectator*'s figures of circulating talk thus provide this writer with a powerful way of imagining and addressing an anonymous and engaged readership. But they do not present any image of that readership engaged in specific political discussion, either strategic or theoretical. Political discussion is still pictured generally as divisive, "low," and "nonsensical."

Political essays published in midcentury newspapers frequently invested political discourse with these attributes. A characteristic beginning for such an essay was a coffeehouse scene and a condemnation of newspapers themselves. It is this set of terms that frames the epigraph for this chapter: "being an idle man, I am a great lounger in Coffeehouses, and a constant reader of all News Papers. . . ."[26] Imagining political discourse, in such formulations, is imagining a continuous, circulating sound in need of regulation by the distancing and disinterested figures of print.

2

Creating a Clamor: The Language of Court Politics

LIKE COFFEEHOUSES, DRAWING ROOMS PROLIFERATED IN EIGHTEENTH-century political writing. They served, for writers interested in describing political participation, as emblematic scenes for the jockeying for position so central to the patronage politics of the court. The local and specific Drawing Room imitated by all the others, and always written with capital letters to indicate its primacy, was the king's. The men and women who received his patronage there went home to their own houses and, at their own levees, distributed smaller posts and rewards to their own dependents. The letters, diaries, and memoirs of courtiers reveal a well-developed language for describing the replication of such scenes and the circulation of news about them to a group referred to as "the public" or, often, "the world." Newspapers, too, employed this language, reporting upon what had been whispered to whom, and what complaints had been provoked in response. British newspapers of the eighteenth century do not describe the focus of the public moving from the court to the town, as in Jürgen Habermas's account of these years.[1] Instead, they depict the public moving to the periphery of the court, where readers were invited to participate at a distance in politics as practiced by the king and his courtiers. Newspapers created an image of their readers eavesdropping at the palace, rather than declaiming in the public square.

The familiar language of business as usual around the court made the abstract process of commodifying and circulating information comprehensible to the people engaged in developing the institutions of the press and the public sphere. This language, however, shaped participation and knowledge around traditional expectations and relationships associated with alliance, loyalty, and patronage. At court, members of the royal family, their attendants, officials, members of Parliament, hangers-on, and servants made policy, carried it out, distributed patronage, and worked to accumulate honor and money for their families. They did so through venerable and highly formal practices of talk and behavior: long visits, charming conversations, smiles and frowns, negotiations, promises, and complaints. This was not the sort of cultural common sense that people practice without being aware of it. Instead, the manners and strategies of courtly behavior had names and were taught to young men and women by their more experienced allies or patrons. The Earl of Chesterfield's letters are the most familiar examples of this common form of instruction that was practiced both orally and in writing. In such writing, we can identify the features of courtly talk that were most important to the participants. Terms such as "information" and "clamour" figured the relationship between replicated drawing-room spaces and the gossip circulated among them. Like "coffee-house talk," these terms indicated an understanding of courtly institutions as media for political participation.

Information and clamor were circulated at and around the levees of powerful men and women. Just as republican political life is often imagined through the ideal of public debate in a space modeled on the Roman Forum, courtly political life was imagined through the ideal of elegant conversation in a levee. The goal of any conversation was to get positive attention, or "favor," from the most powerful person in the room. This was done through displaying "ease," "complaisance," and "parts," so that the king or minister was charmed, amused, or helped out of a difficulty. Successful courtiers were, as the second Earl Waldegrave put it in his memoir, "caress'd in the most public manner; and were honor'd with all the nonsense of gracious smiles, mysterious Nods, and endless Whispers, in every corner of the Drawing Room."[2] Waldegrave was less apt to describe such favors as "nonsense" when he was receiving them himself, rather than watching others receive them as in this passage. Such displays of favor could be turned, eventually, into material favors: offices with pensions or sinecures, marriages for daughters, beneficial tariff measures.

Because the rewards of favor could be so great, the drawing rooms of important people were often thronged during their levees. The size of the crowd at a levee thus indicated the influence of its central figure. When George III appointed the Earl of Bute as first minister, superseding the Duke of Newcastle, who had served his grandfather, petitioners and negotiators flocked to Bute's drawing room. Horace Walpole reported to a friend that Bute's "first levee was crowded. Bothmar, the Danish minister, said, 'La chaleur est excessive.' George Selwyn replied, 'Pour se mettre au froid, il faut aller chez Monsieur le Duc de Newcastle.'" (Bothmar complained that the heat was excessive, and Selwyn replied that to be cool, one should visit the Duke of Newcastle).[3] Selwyn's bon mot was worth repeating for several reasons: it expressed, pithily and in French, the situation of political fortunes. Enduring the heat and discomfort of the new favorite's levee, courtiers might wish for cooler conditions but not enough to join the ousted and powerless Newcastle in his own thinly attended room. Such a comment contained the sort of news courtiers called "information," and traded intensively, using networks of oral, manuscript, and eventually printed communication.

The extent to which this language of courtly politics explicitly referred to its own status as a medium of circulation can be seen in Waldegrave's memoir. In one passage, Waldegrave recalls the tense moment for all courtiers when the young George III took the throne. The men who had served George II expected to be deprived of their jobs (and the pensions and privileges that went with them) to make way for the new king's supporters. Waldegrave describes the night before the coronation. Courtiers waiting in an outer room watch as footmen come out to invite one man after another into the new king's closet for private conversations: "The King did not appear in public but the Duke of Newcastle, the two Secretaries of State, and such Cabinet Counsellors who had not been at Council the preceding day had private Audiences. It was observed that the Earl of Bute was some minutes with his Majesty before each Audience."[4] An observer of this series of meetings could learn a great deal even without meeting the king himself and without any knowledge of what had been said in any of the meetings. Observers like Waldegrave could tell that Bute, the young king's former tutor and best friend, was preparing him for each meeting. He was already functioning as the king's first minister, although none of the old ministers had yet been dismissed. Thus the king's disposition and plans were visible to the people in the outer chamber. News about his conversations would be circulated as people chose to form alliances with or against the newly powerful man.

This passage draws a distinction between the different rooms the king inhabited and the different meanings that could be gained from his tones and looks in each room. Both Hampton Court and St. James's, the two most common places for the court to assemble, contained series of rooms. The private rooms for the royal family, including the king's closet, communicated with a "Drawing Room" and several outer audience rooms. One had to be invited into the king's closet. The Drawing Room, on the other hand, was open to anyone who could get past the footmen at the doors. The footmen judged entrants solely by carefully prescribed standards of dress.[5] Although Britain no longer had sumptuary laws by the eighteenth century and some of the people who could afford such clothes were not technically members of the aristocracy, the group in a court drawing room was assembled and organized by rank and by wealth.

Many of the watchers on this day and on less important days had careers, reputations, and financial futures at stake. Men who held posts like chancellor of the exchequer, privy counselor, or secretary of state could gather enormous influence in Parliament through distributing the smaller posts that came with these departments. The men to whom they gave jobs and pensions could be counted upon to vote with them in Parliament and thus they could make laws and shape national and international policy. More ceremonial posts such groom of the stole or lady in waiting to the queen did not provide access to parliamentary influence, but still allowed the officeholder to distribute jobs, money, and favors and thus to gain influence among a smaller number of friends and relations.[6]

"Information" was the specialized term for news about who had spent time with the king and been treated with favor. Waldegrave provides an example of the precise usage of this term in a description of an earlier time, 1756, during the reign of George II. Frederick, the Prince of Wales, disputing with the king over money, had set up a competing court at Leicester House. Everyone at court had to choose whether to display loyalty to the reigning king or to transfer loyalty to his heir. The king asked Waldegrave to attend at Leicester House and report back upon what was said and done there. Waldegrave records in his memoir a complaint from Frederick, who resented Waldegrave's constant observation of his behavior and daily reports to the king. Waldegrave's account of his answer to this charge uses the term "information" to describe courtly conversations and treats the world surrounding the court as a medium for spreading such information. He writes that he told the prince: "the King having appointed me . . . I was accountable to his Majesty, and it was my Duty to give Informations as to some particulars, when he required it."[7] Even though the prince does not want him, in other words, Waldegrave can attend the prince's levees, observe what goes on, and report back to the king. The king or the prince, then, could not entirely control the makeup of the crowd in the Drawing Room or the use that would be made of the information gathered there.

Once it left the Drawing Room, this information would be spread widely, as Waldegrave goes on to explain in his answer to the prince's complaint: "or supposing it had been my Intention to deceive the King [by keeping information from him], even in that case it would have been absurd to have denied those things, which might be seen at every Drawing room, and were the subject of conversation at every Coffee House."[8] This passage makes clear the connection between events at the most important levees and the lesser political conversations around the city and around the empire. What happened at the prince's Drawing Room displayed political alliances. People in the room and all over the kingdom were choosing between remaining loyal to George II and shifting their allegiance to the Prince of Wales. As influential men and women made this choice, the people who relied upon them and would ask them for favors were faced with similar choices. Thus even country curates, low-ranking army officers, poets and dramatists, tailors, and others who could never hope to attend a court drawing room would have a lively interest in what had taken place there. As they sat in coffeehouses in London, they listened closely to and passed on any news about who had spoken to Prince Frederick, and who had been "caressed" or had a long session of "mysterious whispers" in the Drawing Room.

The audience for drawing-room conversation, then, shared many attributes with the audience for coffeehouse talk or newspaper writing: it was extensive, growing, and treated explicitly as an audience. Discourse addressed to it spread somewhat predictably but not controllably through oral, written, and printed media. Waldegrave uses the term with some care when he writes that the king did not appear "in public." This public fits within the definition proposed by Michael Warner: "a body of strangers united through the circulation of their discourse."[9] The language of drawing-room information figures that public by indicating repeated conversations circulating court news, just as coffeehouse talk indicated conversations circulating bon mots and cultural criticism. Waldegrave's comment above assumes an overlap between the two worlds. In each case, a series of spaces and a medium for circulating discourse among them is indicated by a general phrase pointing to an abstract, public, social phenomenon.

The courtly public figured by Waldegrave's language provides an interesting test case for theories of the public sphere. Warner defines "public" as carefully as he does in the quotation above as part of a larger project, that of separating the concept of publicness from the bourgeois identities and activities usually associated with it. This revision of Habermas and Kant would, he argues, make the concept of publicness politically available for new groups and sensibilities. By arguing for a court-based concept of publicity, I am suggesting that even in the eighteenth century, bourgeois forms were not necessary preconditions for a public sphere. Waldegrave's "public" corresponds neither with Habermas's bourgeois public sphere nor with the "courtly publicity" he identifies in the High Middle Ages. In this model, "the attributes of lordship, such as the ducal seal, were called 'public'. . . . This *publicness* (or *publicity*) *of representation* was not constituted as a social realm, that is, as a public sphere; rather, it was something like a status attribute." The king or lord himself displayed authority, thereby representing the realm. This publicity was "inseperable from the lord's concrete existence, that, as an 'aura,' surrounded and endowed his authority."[10] Waldegrave's careful notes on the inclinations of his prince and king might suggest such a view of authority, but his language of information suggests a different definition of "public," one much closer to Warner's. What is public, in these characteristic descriptions of the Georgian court, is what circulates among the nation's drawing rooms. It is the king's patronage, rather than his aura, which structures this circulation.

The figurative public we can identify in the language of information is neither a lordly aura nor a concept of a civil society made up of "entrepreneurs, manufacturers, and factory owners" who "were affected in their daily existence as consumers by the regulations" of the state, in Habermas's words.[11] He describes a historical succession, from the "representative publicity" of lords to the bourgeois public sphere. The courtly public Waldegrave indicates is, I argue, neither of these. Nor is it a residual form of the dying old order in the process of being superseded by the new. Instead, it should be viewed as a figure useful for making sense of an increasingly large and abstract social world. Although it remained hierarchical and its language and forms remained traditional, the Georgian court was in the process of developing a bureaucracy to administer a global empire and a modern state. The number of people, spaces, and records involved grew as the century went on. Information provided a figure for comprehending these people as a group related by their circulating discourse.

The examples from Waldegrave's memoir suggest the extent to which courtly spaces, like the urban spaces discussed in chapter 1, were treated as a growing system of similar rooms, connected by the circulation of discourse among them. Turning to letters written by participants in this system, we can focus more closely on that circulation and on the role of oral, printed, and written media within it. In the autumn of 1756, Horace Walpole wrote a letter to his friend Henry Fox (later Lord Holland). Fox was engaged in a series of negotiations with the king; he wanted an office, but only if his friends and allies would also be employed and his enemies dismissed. On the morning of October 27, he had a private conversation with the king. Walpole talked with several people later in the day and wrote to Fox:

> After what you know this morning, it would be impertinent in me to tell you what I heard. I only trouble you with this, to apprise you of one thing which you certainly ought to know. The K[ing], Lady Y[armouth], and the Chancellor are persuaded that you would not take the Treasury. I should hope you had made no such resolution. You may depend upon this information.
>
> I know another very particular circumstance, which not being immediately necessary, I should choose not to put upon paper; but if you will give me leave, I will see you in the evening and tell it you.[12]

Walpole begins by explicitly recognizing the superior authority of information gained at a private interview with the king, disowning any intention of being "impertinent" by providing less authoritative information. His own information, however, also comes from the king, although at several removes, and because it may be of use in the next day's negotiations, he provides it: Fox should ask for the office of first lord of the treasury.

The second paragraph of this passage indicates the density of these conversations in the rhythm of the court day. Fox met with the king in the morning; Walpole talked with enough people to hear about this meeting and also to gather supplementary information; Walpole then went home or to his club to write a letter to Fox proposing a meeting for further discussion of the matter. The many other people whose jobs depended upon whether Fox and the king could work out an accommodation were also meeting with the king, with Fox, with Pitt (another possible member of this administration), and with each other. Walpole's letter circulates information he has gathered and suggests a meeting to, perhaps, create a message that he and Fox together can spread further, knowing that it will find its way back to the king. They can rely, in other words, on the other participants in the system continuing to seek and circulate information until all the open offices have been filled. In quite another context, Warner describes this reliance as an aspect of the public culture created by daily newspapers and other modern media: "the punctual time of circulation is crucial to the sense that discussion is currently unfolding in a sphere of activity."[13]

The "punctual time of circulation," which was created in a bourgeois public sphere by periodical print, was created for this courtly public by the social institutions of elite life. Servants ran messages around town at all hours of the day; the expected rituals of luncheon, tea, dinner, and cards provided opportunities to create and circulate expressions of regard, alliance, and confidence. Walpole's mention of Lady Yarmouth, George II's mistress, indicates that women, often excluded from the public in the bourgeois social imagination, played active parts in the courtly public. The social occasions they organized and maintained served as media, the "sphere of activity" for this circulation. Elizabeth Grenville, for instance, wrote her husband George a political letter in December 1755, several weeks before giving birth to a son. She began apologetically: "I believe you must content yourself, my dearest love, to know nothing by this post but what relates to your own fireside, for since your going, I have seen nobody able to give me the least information that I can depend upon, but if the card table to-night furnishes me with any materials, they shall be added in a postscript."[14] We can assume that the card party was productive, because the letter ends with several paragraphs of political news: the speaker of the House waited for a writ from Mr. Hume Campbell, but it never appeared and so the House was adjourned; several people had taken new offices, others remained "unprovided as yet."

This letter suggests the extent to which the social lives of people connected with government were organized around gathering information. At afternoon tea, at dinner, and at cards, both men and women met to socialize but also to compare stories and allow those stories to collect "credit," if they could stand up to the process of being tested against what other people had heard at other gatherings. Even a visibly pregnant woman, if she was married to a politically active man, participated in this process of information gathering at social occasions.

The language of the court can be seen as a public language in the way it relies on and names this sense of a series of spaces into which discourse can be circulated with speed. Using this language was the way to get work done within a patronage system. Holland used the public language in this way in 1765, when a change of ministries cost him his office. When he was dismissed, his appointees at the pay office could have been fired too, to make way for friends and supporters of the new paymaster. Instead, Charles Townshend let them all stay. Holland wrote to Walpole "let me beg of you to show your love to me, by expressing your sense of Mr. Townshend's behavior to me. . . . My brother could not have been more obliging. And nobody can be more obliged than I am, which I beg you and every friend I have, dear Sir, to help me in expressing."[15] Friendship involves patronage and alliance, as well as participation in the network of spreading information. It is important for Townshend to hear of Lord Holland's gratitude not only from Holland himself but from "every friend I have." This way praise of Townshend will be audible in many different rooms all over the West End. The sound will reward Townshend for his noble action and suggest the extent of possible support for him in the future.

Holland used a manuscript letter to create a particular sound, an echoing repetition of his gratitude. Terms for such echoing repetition played a central role in the language of the courtly public. The most commonly used of these terms was "clamour." This word expressed the importance of the repetition or echo, which repeated the same message in different spaces, as well as the hierarchical nature of the system, in which most messages expressed requests, complaints, or gratitude. The records kept by participants in the court world are full of this term. In November 1760, for instance, George Grenville, a member of Parliament and the treasurer of the Navy, received a letter from Charles Jenkinson, a less influential man who often helped Grenville by providing him with political information.[16] "I hear," Jenkinson wrote, "that Lord George Sackville has been at court, and that the King was civil to him. I have much to say to you on this head, which has, I find, already created a clamour, and may possibly create still more, which makes me extremely sorry for it."[17] This bit of gossip was meaningful to Grenville because it made use of familiar terms through which the king communicated with his courtiers and those courtiers communicated with their allies and opponents. King George III, newly crowned that November, was making his interests and preferences clear. He was not a supporter of the Seven Years' War, and he chose to let people know that by being "civil" to Sackville, who had been court-martialed for refusing to attack in the Battle of Minden. The ministers who had carried on the war under George II correctly read the new king's cordiality to Sackville as a gesture of independence from them. The clamor was their orchestrated response, a collection of complaints, whispers, conjectures, and denunciations at dinner tables and coffeehouses around the city that would show George III the strength of their group. The information in Jenkinson's letter would allow Grenville to join in the clamor or to plan a response to it.

Jenkinson's assurance about what constituted important information, how that information was circulated, and how to name and understand the audience for that information, came from his familiarity with the court world's system for circulating and interpreting information. Kings moved between competing groups, organized through family alliances and centered on influential men. It was the king's prerogative to hand out lucrative jobs, but he also had to fill the positions that kept the government working. As we have already seen, men with large and complex groups of allies would often refuse to take jobs unless all their friends were also rewarded and their enemies dismissed. The "outs" waited at their country estates, watching for a change in the emotional and political atmosphere, ready to take office and become "ins." While they waited, they sent lower-ranking friends and allies to London to stand around the Drawing Room and gather information. In the process of demanding better treatment or different policies participants created clamor—the echoing noise of their complaints, articulated at dinners and visits all over the city. The density of sound increased at times when a minister was unhappy with his treatment and resigned, taking his friends and allies with him.

These clamorous changes of administration happened periodically in the reigns of the first two Georges. When George III took the throne, however, he insisted upon giving the office of first minister his good friend the Earl of Bute, who was unpopular and Scottish and had few allies among the important men and women in England. Bute's position in government, combined with the divisions among his enemies, produced a situation where no administration could stay in office very long. It was impossible for any group of ministers to get along with each other, with their own allies, and with Bute and the king. The king was forced to put together new administrations more than five times between 1762 and 1770, and each time the whole system of circulating information and clamoring for notice sprang to life.[18]

In June of 1765, for instance, George Grenville was first minister, Bute having been forced out by his unpopularity. Grenville was not much more popular, however, and the king himself detested him. Various parties in opposition to Grenville were working to form a coalition party and the king was trying to convince William Pitt, who had resigned in 1761, to come back into power as a minister. The Marquess of Rockingham and the Dukes of Newcastle and Devonshire hoped to get into power and thought perhaps that they could do so in alliance with Pitt.

One of the many people watching events closely was thirty-four-year-old Edmund Burke, who had just lost his job as a private secretary. Burke needed a job and a political patron and wrote to several of the possible new ministers, indicating his usefulness by providing information.[19] His letter to Charles Townshend, who had a minor part in the old administration and might have a larger part in the new, described the situation this way:

> I am no wise concerned, that you are not in Town at present. The Scene so far as I can judge of it would not please you a whit the better for your seeing it in a nearer point of View. Mr Pitts stile of acting may be very noble, but it certainly has not been very pleasing. I found, for the few hours I was in Town this morning, most people who used to be tolerably well informed, entirely at a Loss, and not very well satisfied that they were so. Mr P. has very little consulted the leading men in opposition; and both the D. of Newcastle and the Devonshire Set are grievously offended, not only at the real want of confidence, but at the want of respect, in not preserving in the Eyes of the world, the least appearances of it.[20]

We can gather from this account that immediately upon arriving in London, Burke has visited particular people, expecting to learn from them about Pitt's plans and about their own judgments of what will be happening in the near future. These people are embarrassed by their inability to offer this sort of information to Burke and to other visitors who have come on the same errand.

Pitt's motives in this course of action remain somewhat murky, although bouts of debilitating depression, alternating with good health, appear to have caused some of the vacillations that so confused contemporaries. At the time, as a biographer of Pitt writes, "much . . . political industry . . . was devoted to attempts at interpreting Pitt's motives."[21] Burke's description of Pitt's "style of acting" shows how much politicians paid attention to conversations themselves, as well as their content. The Dukes of Devonshire and Newcastle, in Burke's account, are humiliated because they have been deprived of information to circulate. If they had been "consulted" by Pitt at all, they would have been able to pass on information to Burke and other callers, implying if not promising that Pitt had invited them to make up an administration. Pitt, Burke implies, would not have had to promise anything or to divulge any information. The "consultation," however, would have given the other men a chance to make suggestions or requests and to show their own followers that they were men of consequence. In avoiding them, Pitt has acted as if their support is unnecessary to him, slighting them and their followers.

A month after Burke wrote this letter, Grenville's supporters made a claim for their own consequence on the same grounds—they were important because they had been consulted by Pitt. Horace Walpole wrote to Lord Holland on July 19 that "the . . . ministers brag of a visit Mr. Pitt has made to Geo. Grenville, which lasted long enough for one of them to have made a speech in, in short, four hours."[22] Walpole, not a supporter of Grenville, communicated this information because it might be of use to his friend, even as he denigrated it as "bragging" and suggested that even such a long visit could be as empty as a long-winded speech. As in many of the other examples of information I have quoted, the content of this conversation is not as important to the participants and their friends as its length.

In these letters, Burke and Walpole were participating not just in gathering information, but in spreading it further and in reacting to it according to their own loyalties and interests. Burke wrote to Townshend about Pitt's slighting of the members of the opposition not just to explain that it had happened, but to explain how unhappy those men were. If Burke was not the only person working to make himself useful to this group of men, as it is likely he was not, then other conversations and letters reported on the unhappiness of Devonshire and Newcastle. Pitt would have many opportunities to hear about this unhappiness, as he visited and dined around the city, and could judge the opposition's strength by the number of times he heard about their injured feelings. Like the gratitude Holland asked his friends to express, these complaints would echo, forming a repeated sound—clamor.

The *Oxford English Dictionary*'s definition of clamor emphasizes its association with complaint: "loud shouting or outcry, vociferation; esp. the excited outcry of vehement appeal, complaint, or opposition; commonly, but not always, implying a mingling of voices." The early uses cited in the *OED* come from the cries of animals ("the clamour of the craving nest") bells, and grieving women. As early as 1483, however, Caxton used it to describe people making requests of God: "Our Lord God . . . forgetteth not the clamour and prayer of the trewe and juste." This use suggests a request to a sovereign from a group, just as the letters of Burke and Walpole did. By the mid-nineteenth century, the word had come to mean vociferous popular opinion, as when crowds clamor for justice. In the eighteenth century, however, the word was caught up in the particular system of courtly communication I have been describing and was meaningful inside that system. When Charles Jenkinson wrote to Grenville that the king's civility to Sir George Sackville had "occasioned clamour," he did not suggest a mass uprising or a riot or even a flood of newspaper editorials. Instead, he referred to a series of angry conversations in drawing rooms and over dinner tables all over the city, conversations that would eventually get back to the king to let him know he had shown civility to an unpopular man.

Clamor, in this sense of a noise that echoes because the same sentiments are being voiced in multiple conversations on the same day, had been familiar to courtiers at least since the reign of Queen Anne, and Caxton's use of the term suggests an even earlier date. Its importance in this system and in speakers' conceptions of their audiences can be seen in an account from John Hervey's memoir of political life under George I. Hervey describes a conversation that took place in 1732, between the prime minister, Robert Walpole, and the bishop of Salisbury. The bishop, a member of Parliament, wanted to bring a bill before Parliament proposing that dissenters be given the right to vote. Walpole, before talking to the bishop, "had sounded many of the firmest friends to the Government upon this point, and found so many against it in opinion . . . and so many more against it for prudential and personal reasons with regard to their interest in the country, that he was sure, if the point was now to be tried, it could not be carried. . . ." The "firmest friends to the government" were members of Parliament who consistently voted in the ways that the king and his ministers asked them to. Even these men, however, were not unified behind the measure. Some opposed it and others found that their own supporters, people they needed to keep their seats in parliament, opposed it. Walpole knew that it would never pass and, even worse for him, it would expose his supporters to a divisive vote and let everyone know who had voted with him and who had not.

Rather than show weakness in this way, Walpole refused to allow the bishop to bring the bill at all. Hervey reports that Walpole told the bishop: "As to himself, in private and in confidence, he would not scruple to own to the Bishop that his heart was with them; but in this country, which was in reality a popular government that only bore the name of monarchy, and especially in this age where clamour and faction were so prevalent over reason and justice, he said a minister sometimes must swim with the tide against his inclination, and that the current was too strong at present against this proposal of the Dissenters for any judicious minister to think of stemming it."[23] This account of the situation makes clear the place that clamor had in court decision making. Walpole is claiming that if he endorses the bill, he will hear clamor from factions opposed to it. His claim that the country "was in reality a popular government" does not refer to a state governed by and for the people. He refers only to members of Parliament, many of whom received fat pensions from him, and to their "interest in the country," their ability to please the landowning voters and influential families in their home counties. Clamor, in this passage, would be the oral response of this group of members of Parliament and their supporters, faced with a measure they did not like. Knowing which card tables and dinners were the right conduits back to Walpole, these people would express their unhappiness and know that it would be repeated wherever Walpole went in town. His enemies, too, would hear the complaints and be able to judge which of his usual supporters were less firmly loyal to him than the others, which supporters might be led to abandon their alliance to him for a new one.

Although they did not consider themselves to be engaged in literary activity, the members of the court world were intensely interested in forms and in media. They spoke and listened in ways that made sense within the system of conversations surrounding the court. When they listened they were aware of degrees of graciousness, of civility, of cordiality. When they spoke they worked to charm, indulged in what Waldegrave called "Panegyrick," traded "information," and generated "clamour."[24] Along with these forms, speakers and listeners were aware of the media through with they communicated. They sent messages through the system, knowing with some accuracy how and where they would be received.

A record of a conversation was important in the court world only if it could represent sound and produce more sound, in a process of replication and circulation. Because one did not walk into the Drawing Room with a sheaf of papers but with a sword or fan, all documents had eventually to be translated back into sound. Although the participants in this system made use of manuscript and print to store and circulate their discourse, it is important to note that the metaphors in this writing are all oral. It is the situation of the conversation, the smiles, and the tones of voice that are meaningful. When people actually use writing for its convenience and permanence, they do not cease to frame their understandings of political events in figures based on speech. When thinking about "cultures" of orality, manuscript, or print, then, it is important to attend not only to the uses of those media but to the figurations created from those media. In this case, the Georgian court can in no way be described as an "oral culture" in the terms used by anthropologists.[25] The people whose letters I have been quoting were members of an elite, highly literate group in the process of creating a global empire based at least in part upon printed money. However, for them, cultural and political significance was attached not to the media they used at one time or another, but to the media that served as figures abstracting a particular linguistic exchange into an example of a general phenomenon. In this case, courtly publics are made through abstracting conversations about the moods and inclinations of the powerful into a social order made up of more and less skilled observers and negotiators. For everyday political use, people reported on what their friends and acquaintances were saying, rather than on what they read in their letters. Whatever medium was actually used, figures of speech based on echoing sounds structured the language of politics.

Because oral figures carried political significance, writers with access to both manuscript and print continued to describe political events in oral terms. Although Horace Walpole owned his own printing press and wrote enough manuscript letters to fill thirty-six volumes in the Yale edition, for instance, he often used oral figures to describe political situations. In a letter to Lord Holland written in 1765, he summed up Holland's political options through repeating the comments members of different factions had made about him:

> Lord Halifax and Lord Sandwich may be as guilty to you as the rest of the crew, but I cannot say that I have heard them particularly named. At Bedford House their violence against you is boasted of, and they have even been so brutal as to say it would kill you, though I thought they knew your spirit a little better. George Grenville's share in it you cannot doubt, from his own malice to you, and from the new fuel which his brother Temple has supplied. I was told at Richmond House that the Junto had proposed to dismiss you in a very ignominious manner. . . . I cannot mention this dirty spite, without doing justice to the Duke of Richmond, who resents this treatment of you in the warmest, most open, and most friendly manner. Lord Bute, you know, I am not acquainted with; but by what I see in his friends, he is thoroughly enraged. . . .[26]

It is clear from this passage that great houses were institutions for the creation and circulation of information. At his own house, the Duke of

Richmond has "resented" the treatment of Lord Holland. In other words, he has spoken in protest in front of people who he knows will repeat his words. Speaking in front of this audience in his own house is called by Walpole an "open manner." He has emphasized his opinion by being "warm" and "friendly" to Walpole, known by everyone to be a close friend of Holland. This tone works as a declaration of independence from Grenville and the people at Bedford House.

None of the expressions of emotion Walpole describes, whether warm, friendly, or enraged, are simply individual or personal. They are all declarations of allegiance or independence—thus Lord Bute's emotions can be judged by "what I see in his friends." Friendship was a matter of correctly reading and passing on information contained in tones and contexts, as well as particular words. Lord Holland knew from this letter that the Duke of Richmond was his friend, as well as that Horace Walpole was.

The specificity with which eighteenth-century court insiders used terms such as "clamour" and "information" suggests the extent to which they were self-consciously figuring the courtly language as a system. Clamor was a figure of speech because it connected speeches heard in different rooms into a single sound. The figure of the echo central to the word expressed this connection, indicating the understanding that sounds heard in different places derived their meanings from their relations to each other. Because of its influence, this system was familiar to people all over the nation, even people distant from the court by birth or inclination. The forms and media of court communication served as a way of thinking about the reproduction and transmission of information both for courtiers and for speakers and writers with quite different projects. The eighteenth-century newspaper-reading public learned to think of itself as such through practicing the familiar forms of gossip that had surrounded the English court for a century or more. As they read and wrote letters and read and printed newspapers, they conveyed information about the disposition of powerful people, about what "everyone was saying" in certain sections of town, and about the chat in coffeehouses. These practices provided media and familiar forms, even for writers and politicians interested in alternatives to the court, rank, and ease as sources of authority in political life.

Turning from manuscript to newspaper writing, we can identify the same conventions in operation. Newspapers reported what "we hear" and what "is said," not only because those were familiar ways of indicating communication but because such hearing and saying were themselves news. If a powerful person's civility was a sign of an impending change in policy, as George III's civility to Sackville was, then what was heard near the centers of power, even in social conversation, was important information for anyone interested in war and peace, taxation, trade, or offices. If repeated comments constituted clamor, and clamor was a demonstration of power by one alliance or another, then what was heard, and especially what was heard more than once, was important information for anyone trying to make plans based on who might be in what office in the future.

In making this argument, I am examining a tension that has been noticed by several scholars of the eighteenth-century press and politics. As Jeremy Black has put it, although scholars no longer write "political history that explains everything simply in terms of the activities of the Duke of Newcastle and five others," the political writing of important ministers and members of Parliament tends to ignore public opinion almost entirely.[27] Readers of eighteenth-century papers are often struck by the growing vigor of popular political life in this period and the irrelevance of that life to the day-to-day running of the state by a small elite. Hannah Barker points out that "the public" was often addressed and discussed by the period's newspaper writers, but was not seen as a revolutionary political force: "these individuals were thought to have a legitimate interest in the public affairs of their nation, which they could pursue and express without challenging the broad constitutional structures within which they lived." She identifies an effective and self-conscious "public opinion" expressed in newspapers quite late in the century, "between 1779 and 1785," at which point weekly newspapers had been familiar in London for seventy years and cheap, printed, political comment for closer to one hundred.[28] Midcentury newspapers make interesting reading precisely because they suggest how contemporaries understood and negotiated the apparent conflict between a vibrant popular political culture and that culture's practical separation from political structures.[29]

Although London newspapers were available to a socially and geographically wide readership, they often reported on levees, balls, and other scenes of aristocratic display.[30] Often the news columns began with paragraphs such as these, from the *London Chronicle* for January 22, 1767:

> Last night the Duchess of Northumberland had a great rout at Northumberland House. Invitations were given to above four hundred of the Nobility.

Yesterday the Earl of Tyrone arrived at his house in Pall-Mall, from Ireland.

. . .

His Grace the Duke of Bedford yesterday distributed to the poor sort of people in Covent Garden 50 l. by the hands of the Lessee of the said market.

In each case, these events are newsworthy because they demonstrate the power and influence of courtly figures and the constellations of loyalty and attachment that surround them.

When important events took place around the court, the pace and volume of such reports increased dramatically. A paragraph in the *London Chronicle* commented on the many changes of administration during the 1760s by describing a new edition of the court calendar, which listed all officials and their offices. The new edition, the writer quipped, "will be published on Asses Skin, for the convenience of rubbing out and replacing of names; since the printed lists will be useless, if not renewed once a month at least."[31] This newspaper writer does not make much of print's replicability and ephemerality, as historians of print have done. Instead, the paragraph treats a printed copy of the calendar as a semipermanent record. Ass's skin serves the satirical purpose of relating jackasses and politics, of course. But it also suggests that the changing fortunes of families and factions were understood as phenomena difficult to capture in writing. The offices were fixed and immutable, but the officeholders were frequently rubbed out and replaced.

The summer of 1765 provides a particularly revealing example of newspaper reporting on such courtly events. After months of conflict between the king and his first minister, George Grenville, a new ministry was put together in July. Grafton and Rockingham were in; Grenville was out. The crowds flowed to the levees of the newly powerful, leaving the members of the former ministry to retire to their country seats with only their closest allies. The London section of the *London Chronicle* for July 25, 1765 began with the following paragraphs:

We are told that on the first rumour of the late changes, a celebrated Commoner wrote a letter to a great Lawyer, which was to the following *purport* or *tenor*.

"Sir, I am informed that you are shortly to be removed from your office, and it is reported that I am the adviser of your removal—I deny it. On the contrary, did the circumstances of the times allow me to take a post in the administration, I would think myself happy in the assistance of a person, in that high office, of your experience and abilities. I am, Sir, &c."

. . .

It is said that the Secretary to— —is a strongly *suspected* Roman Catholic. His brother was a *known* Papist, and in the late rebellion.

It is reported that when the new M— —y was settling, the D. of N. told the M. of R. that he must be F— —st L— —of the T. His Lordship objected on account of his *inexperience*. "It does not signify, my Lord, (replied his G— —) F—st L— —of the T. you must be. Care will be taken to appoint proper persons to assist your Lordship in the *business* of your department; and as to the disposal of the *places* in your Lordship's power, if you think you are not qualified *there,* I am ready to undertake *that* part of your office myself."

The typographical emphases and evasions of this passage, which make it almost opaque to a twenty-first century reader, referred directly, for an eighteenth-century reader, to a series of voices repeating political information. The dashes and nicknames serve partly to protect the printer from libel charges. But they also serve to mark insider knowledge and provide readers with opportunities for showing off their interpretive skills. William Pitt, the "Great Commoner," was known throughout the nation, and many people had hoped he would accept a post in the new administration. Coffeehouse or tea-table readers could fill in the blanks, identifying Pitt and reconstructing the Duke of Newcastle's conversation with the Marquess of Rockingham about taking the office of first lord of the treasury.

The paragraph describing the letter from Pitt combines genres and media in a precise and layered way. It begins with claiming to report what "we are told." This report, in other words, has reached the offices of the *London Chronicle* through unnamed channels. The paragraph then quotes from a private letter, written in manuscript for an individual reader, and it does so using quotation marks. These would, in a twenty-first-century newspaper, indicate that the writer had copied directly from the manuscript, and that the copy had been checked. Here, however, the quotation marks associate the manuscript letter with the voice of the writer. They do not claim to indicate accuracy, since the entire paragraph reports only what "we are told" and conveys a general "purport or tenor" rather than a specific set of facts.

The "great lawyer" referred to in this paragraph was probably Fletcher Norton, described by one historian as "a lawyer noted for his vigour and his naked ambition," who was dismissed from his office as attorney general on July 19.[32] It was in Norton's interest to inform the political world that Pitt, then the most popular of the possible ministers, supported him. His dismissal might then be seen as a side effect of George Grenville's dispute with the king, rather than as a reflection on Norton's abilities or connections. Publishing an account of such a personal letter of support would extend the common practice of showing letters around among one's friends and acquaintances. This practice mirrored that of passing around accounts of the distribution of favor at court. (A complementary episode can be found in the discussions of Samuel Johnson's letter rejecting the patronage of Lord Chesterfield. This letter has been lost, but it was discussed so often by the friends of both men that Johnson was prevailed upon to dictate a version from memory years later.)[33] A newspaper paragraph reporting a rumor about a private letter written in response to another rumor, then, provided valuable and interesting political information. Its accuracy would be measured by other rumors, by the flow of carriages and crowds from one levee to another, and by the eventual makeup of the new ministry.

The next paragraph in the passage reports on what "is said" rather than what "we are told." By omitting reference to any particular listener as well as to any particular speaker, the paragraph bases its authority upon the claim that such conversation is general. Rather than claiming to have access to an eye witness, the paper claims to report what is available everywhere (in certain privileged circles). The suspected Roman Catholic was probably Edmund Burke, newly hired as secretary to the Marquess of Rockingham. In the following weeks, the *London Chronicle* printed several defenses of Burke, still unnamed, as a gentleman with a high reputation in the literary world and a Protestant education.[34] A suspicion of Catholicism could weaken Rockingham's coalition as members of Parliament considered whether to support his ministry.

The last of these paragraphs is also critical of the new ministry. Reporting on what the Duke of Newcastle might have said to the Marquess of Rockingham, who was young and inexperienced but who was gaining access to enormous sources of patronage through the dismissal of men like Norton and those who worked under them, the paragraph provides opportunities to suspect these two men and the entire system of patronage. Historians have associated such a suspicion of the court and of placeholders with a "country" ideology as opposed to a courtly one. This paragraph does make information available in a form useful for an anticourt critique—how terrible it is, one could easily respond, that all these great men care about is distributing places. What about the business of the nation? If that is performed by underlings, why do these great men receive pensions for their offices?

Notice, however, that the form of this paragraph matches the others very closely. It is framed as a reported speech, perhaps overheard and then retold in quotation marks. The italics mark the emphases not of the original speech but of the critical hearer retelling the story. It is this reporter who wants readers to notice that "places" seem more important than the "business" of the department for these speakers. There are, then, not two but at least three voices represented in the passage. And the critique does not propose, as an alternative to conversations between the duke and the marquess, a reasonable debate about the general good. Instead, it raises, obliquely, the possibility of damaging the reputations of both the duke and the marquess by suggesting that they are not as devoted to their independence as aristocrats should be.

As a group, then, these paragraphs report on a rumor about a private letter, a rumor about a suspicion, and an anecdote about a conversation. Each paragraph measures the rising and falling values of reputations. Repeatedly, the paper makes political information comprehensible by presenting it in the form of conversations between courtly insiders. In this way, newspaper writers treated the patronage and inclinations of powerful figures, and the shifting reactions of less powerful people toward that patronage and those inclinations, as models for all political events. Like the gossip heard in gaming houses and coffeehouses and the information written in manuscript letters, news in these paragraphs circulated outward from the center where decisions were made, requests answered, and arrivals greeted either graciously or otherwise.

Newspapers consistently presented political information in such courtly terms during the first three-quarters of the century. Even when reporting on events outside the houses of important people, newspapers often maintained the forms and conventions of paragraphs like those above, passing on what had been heard, said, and whispered. The *Whitehall Evening Post* for January 10, 1761, ran the following paragraphs:

> We hear that the Government has contracted for 30,000 Ton of Shipping, which is to be got ready with all possible Dispatch, for the Service of an Expedition, which will shortly take Place.
>
> We hear that two Bankers on Friday last, by Commission, bought into the New Subscription 140 000l.
>
> Saturday the Duke and Duchess of Portland came to Town, from their Seat in Buckinghamshire.

> Sunday the Earl of Pembroke, lately arrived from Germany, waited on his Majesty, and was received very graciously.

In this passage, the news that looks today like gossip, accounts of the movements of and relationships between celebrities like the Duke of Portland and the Earl of Pembroke, are *not* marked with a "we hear," while military and financial events *are* marked that way. Events that we can, with hindsight, associate with the growth of a new, market-driven society and a financially and culturally powerful capitalist elite are in these paragraphs described in the same terms as courtly events. Information about the government's military plans and the city of London's financial responses is available and comprehensible through access to powerful figures. The rising and falling fortunes of earls and dukes and their dependents are in this way similar to the rising and falling of stocks or the victories and defeats of wartime.

News paragraphs frequently described information in oral terms, even when it was actually communicated in a manuscript letter to the printer and then in the printed newspaper itself, because the information was understood through the image of the levee. An example of such deliberate use of oral terms can be found in a letter written to Henry Woodfall, the printer of the *Public Advertiser,* by the Earl of Sandwich. Dated February 23, 1773, the letter presents a paragraph for the newspaper:

> Mr. Woodfall,
>
> I shall be obliged to you if without mentioning my name or giving any hint where this comes from, you would, if possible, insert the underwritten paragraph in your paper of tomorrow . . . the fact with regards to the action is true. I am,
>
> Your very humble Servant,
> Sandwich
>
> We hear that the Earl of Sandwich has caused an action to be brought against the printer of the London Evening Post of the 2nd of February, in order to vindicate his honour against the infamous falsehood contained in that paper.[35]

This manuscript letter, then, requests the printer to treat a piece of news as a "we hear" when it actually has been directly received from a reputable source. The earl is engaging in the world of printed news and public opinion by reacting to misinformation printed in a newspaper through a lawsuit (rather than, for instance, challenging the printer to a duel). He participates in this arena of law and print, however, through a paragraph framed in the customary way, through the forms of heard and overheard news. In this way, Sandwich's letter corresponds with the news paragraphs about the new ships ordered by the government and the Duke and Duchess of Portland's visit to town. News, according to this way of thinking, originates at a center of power and takes the form of an original oral exchange. That exchange is repeated in a widening circle of other conversations, in writing, and in print. This widening circle provided a conceptual frame for understanding news even when it did not describe the way an actual piece of news had been gathered, recorded, or disseminated.

Newsworthy events happened in many places, but news about them was described as originating at one center. Both the production and the distribution of news are imagined, in these passages, using aural metaphors that misrepresent the newspapers' empirical situation. Newspapers were actually produced in several places in London, then sent out along the postal routes to other towns, where they were redistributed by newsagents, hawkers, and coffeehouse and tavern owners. In many provincial towns, passages from the London papers were also selectively reprinted, juxtaposed with passages from international papers and accounts of local news.[36] Distribution, then, can be seen as nodal—copies of papers fanned out from London, but provincial centers redirected and redistributed the papers themselves and their contents. There is a conflict between the actual distribution pattern of the papers and the metaphors for distribution used by their writers. News is framed, in the passages I have quoted and in many others, as originating in the West End of London and spreading out from there in a wave with a single center. These passages describe newspaper distribution as amplified sound rather than circulated text. "We hear" is a figure, rather than an empirical description of newspaper production and delivery at midcentury. The widespread use of this figure suggests that despite its inaccuracy it served to make the abstract connections between distant actors, writers, and readers comprehensible.

Newspapers also modeled the forms through which their reading publics could discuss and respond to the news. Scholarly accounts of print culture have imagined these discussions among newspaper readers as the location of a new sort of political discussion: democratic, enlightened, rational. Habermas describes the discussion societies, salons, and coffeehouses where such conversation could be practiced as oriented toward the "town" rather than the "court." In these spaces, the debates "disregarded status altogether. The tendency replaced the celebration of rank with a tact befitting equals. [This tendency created a] parity on whose basis alone the authority of the better argument could assert itself against that of the social hierarchy and in the end carry the day. . . ."[37] Such conversations, according to Habermas, became abstract rather than concrete. Government could be discussed in terms of the rule of law, rather than of a particular king. Specific policies could be evaluated according to the light of reason, rather than according to the particular interests of factions or families. "Public debate was supposed to transform *voluntas* into a *ratio* that in the public competition of private arguments came into being as the consensus about what was practically necessary in the interest of all."[38] Turning a *voluntas,* or will, into a *ratio,* or reasoned judgment, directed political work away from inclinations and toward general laws. To determine "what was practically necessary" in such a conversation, participants would be searching for a course of action in accord with natural laws such as those believed to govern the market, as well as the laws of reason. Such actions, because of their correspondence with impersonal laws, would serve "the interest of all" rather than the interest of any particular group or faction. Many scholars of print culture have followed Elizabeth Eisenstein in associating such discussions with print's capacity for "decontextualizing" information by replicating it in the day's 100 or 1,000 copies of a newspaper and circulating it to people outside the traditional oral networks of information exchange.[39]

The terms Habermas uses are directly opposed to those governing conversations at a levee. Disregarding status, developing "tact," a language for exchanges among equals, and bestowing authority on "the better argument" rather than "the social hierarchy" would not be useful activities to someone trying to understand or affect events at court. They would be counterproductive, since the alliances and obligations structuring the social hierarchy provided the categories through which courtiers worked. That difference suggests, as Habermas points out, how radically new the concept of a public critique of the state could be. The newspaper paragraphs examined above, however, suggest that as late as 1765, many writers in manuscript and in print described coffeehouse culture as an extension of the levee, rather than an alternative to it. Waldegrave's comment quoted above assumes that the material for conversation at "every" coffeehouse in town came from the events that had taken place at the most recent Drawing Room as the king or prince displayed favor. Newspaper writers revealed a similar assumption when they reported upon what was heard and whispered and upon the levees of important people. Such reports assumed that their readers were interpreting information according to forms derived from courtly, rather than rational, models of political information.

Newspapers also indicated the forms their readers' responses and interpretations might take. Because readers were gaining information about events over which they had no influence, their responses were confined to speculation and conjecture. For example, the *Public Advertiser*'s London news for January 15, 1765, included paragraphs reporting that

> It is whispered about the West End of the Town, that the people employed in demolishing the Fortifications of Dunkirk have lately been discharged from that Work.—A Circumstance which must occasion some Speculation.
>
> We hear the intended Marriage of the Hereditary Prince of Denmark with her Royal Highness Princess Louisa of England will soon open a Negotiation for certain new Treaties of Commerce and Defence, between the Courts of Copenhagen and London, of the utmost Benefit to their respective Subjects, and in which a third Maritime Power on the Continent will be invited to join.

The fortifications at Dunkirk were seen as indices of French intentions to resume hostilities or remain at peace after the end of the Seven Years' War. They were rebuilt and demolished many times in the London newspapers. The news about the forts reported here is not only heard but overheard. The paragraph reports upon a whisper in a particular part of town, the West End, closest to the sources of information. It is important to note that this news does not come directly from Dunkirk itself, the location a twenty-first-century reader might expect to provide the best information. For an eighteenth-century reader, the West End of London was a much better source of information because it was physically nearer to powerful people. A reader with information from that part of town was part of a circle of information centered on the king. The whisper in the newspaper provides readers with the illusion of being let in on a secret in the presence of others. This paragraph, then, has the same form as the scene described by Waldegrave, where favorites are whispered to and caressed in every corner of the Drawing Room. This paragraph borrows the gestures of confidence and exclusion from court etiquette, casting the reader in the role of a courtier present in the Drawing Room but at a distance from the powerful figure. In such a place, the reader must observe behavior, attend to whispers, and speculate upon the meaning of the display. The reference to the unnamed "third Maritime Power" plays a similar role—obliqueness gives the reader an opportunity for conjecture based on inside knowledge, or perhaps for a knowing smile or whisper of her own.

The role of such conjecture and speculation in the interpretation of news paragraphs is made explicit in some paragraphs that appeared in the *London Chronicle* for July 18, 1765. A particularly difficult change in ministries was taking place, and the country watched as the important players negotiated: "Thursday Lord Northington was sent for at two o'clock to St. James's. His Lordship was then upon the Bench at Lincoln's-Inn-Hall, which he immediately left. Various were conjectures. His Lordship next day set out for his seat at the Grange." Lord Northington was a trusted confidant of the king, working to put together a ministry the king would favor.[40] Readers could use paragraphs like those about Lord Northington to supplement information about the king's dislike of Grenville, or about Pitt's refusal to take any office at all, and make more accurate, or at least more interesting, "conjectures" than their neighbors who had not read the papers. By reporting visits like Northington's to the king and conjectures upon them, the newspapers participated in this culture of court watching. In doing so, they perpetuated a political culture in which the participation of ordinary people was restricted to conjectures upon the mysterious and fascinating events taking place at court. Political knowledge, when framed by these modes of discussion, was insider knowledge.

Alternative models of political discussion, such as rational deliberation about the public good or theoretical consideration of social contracts, are not acknowledged by these paragraphs. It is not surprising to find that the second Earl Waldegrave or the correspondents of George Grenville did not write in terms Habermas would identify as characteristic of the bourgeois public sphere. A weekly paper like the *London Chronicle,* however, provided material for coffeehouse discussion; we might therefore expect to find its accounts of political events framed in Habermasian terms. The news about Lord Northington quoted above, however, is meaningful only because of his rank. To analyze the paper's information about him in universalist terms, disregarding status, would require one to ignore almost all the information presented in the paragraphs. Information about Northington's loyalty to the king had to be understood in the context of his family's marriages, alliances, and obligations, as well as of his personal charm and sense of honor.

Wars and financial markets, however, could be discussed meaningfully in other ways. They are more general, "social" phenomena, the sort that according to Habermas drew writers and speakers to call upon an abstract realm of reason and law outside the inclinations and histories of individuals. But these paragraphs and many others discuss the economy and the nation's foreign policy as if they too begin in a smile or frown in a drawing room and ripple outward. The "we hears" and "whispers" cause newspaper writers to describe military and economic events as beyond the control of ordinary people, whose participation is rhetorically constructed in the form of conjecture and reaction. The *Public Advertiser* for May 3, 1765, included the following paragraphs:

> We hear an Account of the various Merchandize in the Island of Jersey and Guernsey, subject to the Duties of the Customs and Excise upon their being landed in Great Britain will speedily be ordered for Inspection, previous to certain Resolutions now on the Carpet, respecting the future Trade of both those Islands.
>
> There is now a Talk that most of the Cutters lately taken into the Government's Service to cruize against the Smugglers, will be turned over to the immediate Direction of his Majesty's Officers of the Customs and Exise; by which a Savings of several Thousand Pounds per Annum will be made to the Nation.

This news, unlike the paragraphs about the Marquess of Rockingham's personal secretary or the Duchess of Northumberland's ball, concerns the actions of the customs and excise bureaucracy. The interest of this information is in the "savings" that will be made "to the nation." This is the language of the general good. Such paragraphs suggest the window through which readers and writers might have begun to glimpse possibilities for new and different forms of public political discussion. Keeping track of the actions and arguments of elected representatives differs from watching the maneuvers of courtiers. The writer of these paragraphs considers the expenditures of "his Majesty's officers" as savings "to the Nation," rather than savings simply to His Majesty.

This nod to the general good opens, however, with familiar oral tags: "we hear" and "there is a talk." Both of these paragraphs report actions that were being taken by the state: merchandise "will speedily be ordered for inspection," cutters "will be turned over." These actions are presented as unalterable moves to which readers can react, moving their merchandise out of Jersey or hiding their smuggled goods, rather than as policies available for public discussion. Alternative arguments are not suggested or implied by the form of the paragraphs. Coffee-house discussions of these paragraphs, then, might just as easily be imagined in the familiar forms of courtly gossip as in the rational form described by Habermas.

Two years later, such juxtapositions of economic news and courtly forms were still routine. The *London Chronicle* for May 5, 1767, reported:

> This evening their Majesties go to Drury-lane Theatre to see The School for Lovers, with Lethe, in which Mr. Garrick performs Lord Chalkstone.
>
> We hear that his Excellency the Earl of Bristol will set out in a few days for Parkgate, where a King's yacht now lyes ready to carry his Lordship and his train for Dublin.
>
> This day was held a great board of Trade and Plantations; at which some Merchants trading to the Muskito shore, and other Colony Agents, attended.
>
> This morning his grace the Duke of Grafton had a numerous Levee at Whitehall.

The Board of Trade was made up of the men who administered the British Empire. Here, merchants whose profits and interests would shape the economic and political future of America and of the empire "attend" upon the ministers who make policy. The difficult questions of internal and external taxation, of slavery and disease, and of market expansion associated with trading to the Mosquito Coast go unmentioned. The Duke of Grafton's numerous levee, however, merits its own paragraph.

Such reporting was hardly an intentional conspiracy of aristocratic elites bracing against a capitalist, bourgeois, print-based future. Both the courtiers and the newspaper writers were going about their day-to-day business, using familiar terms, institutions, and technology and adapting new methods as they became available. Reporting political news in terms of rumor and conjecture did, however, perpetuate a concept of political discourse that channeled public discussion. Neither conjecture nor rumor provided tools for determining the "authority of the better argument," in Habermas's terms. Instead, newspapers extended and amplified the circles of talk surrounding the daily political events of the Georgian court. They allowed readers to "overhear" the whispers and reports that constituted political information among the people who surrounded the king, and they provided those readers with ample material for speculation and conjecture.

3

Clamor in the Newspapers: Figurative Publics in Midcentury Newspaper Writing

TWENTY-FIRST-CENTURY NEWSPAPERS CALL UPON THE METAPHORICAL power of aural forms with titles like the *Clarion,* the *Cryer,* or Peter Parker's employer, the *Daily Bugle.* These titles, suggesting courtly and military ritual, are perhaps less compelling today than the visual *Sun* or the abstract and secular *Times.* In the eighteenth century, however, newspapers frequently described their own content in terms of sound: "for some years past people of every rank complained of the dearness of provisions, our News-papers have been filled with these murmurs, and they have almost engrossed every private conversation."[1] Newspapers were filled with more than murmurs; writers frequently characterized their own work as clamor, coffeehouse talk, echoes or shouts. A newspaper can be filled with murmurs only figuratively. The words printed on the page can be understood as murmurs if they indicate restiveness on the part of people to whom leaders are beholden.

For newspapers to make sense to their readers, their writers must be able to call upon a conceptual link between distant events, unknown writers, and anonymous audiences. Benedict Anderson has articulated for us the "imagined" nature of such links. That imaginative work was done, I will argue in this chapter, through an accretion of figures for political talk, not only in titles but in the papers' political commentary. The coffeehouse talk represented by the *Spectator* writers and the clamor invoked by courtly writers served newspaper writers who wanted to imply that their own discourse was widely circulating and influential. These metaphors hold a central place in political theory because they structure the concepts of public voice and public discussion, concepts used to imagine public opinion and the public itself. This chapter argues that the effect of public discussion, the newspapers' representation of an anonymous group of readers engaged among themselves in exploring the importance of day-to-day political events, is an effect of the juxtapositions between metaphors of clamor and coffeehouse chat. Examining those juxtapositions reveals the gaps and spaces between the figures and the actual mechanisms of political representation.

Commentary in eighteenth-century papers was often conveyed through "letters to the printer," written in some cases by a paper's staff, in others by advocates for particular individuals, groups, or policies, and in still others by readers. Over the course of the eighteenth century, these letters recorded the accretion of figures for political talk, as clamor was juxtaposed with coffeehouse chat, complaints, bon mots, and murmurs in the columns of the daily and weekly papers. Clamour provided letter writers with a figure for circulating and influential discourse. Juxtaposing figures based on clamour with figures based on coffeehouse chat, newspapers presented readers with a picture of public life located in a realm of self-referential, figurative, circulating talk. The talk itself is figured in familiar ways, but the arena of such talk as represented in the papers is more flexible, multiple, and critical than the courtly or sociable arenas from which its figures are drawn.

These letters are difficult to explain according to a Habermasian narrative in which the locus of political life moves from the court to the town and from courtly performance to rational discussion, because they continue to describe political talk in terms of clamor, even when addressing an anonymous print public and attempting to influence public opinion. Understanding the changes in political life as occurring through the juxtaposition and accretion of figures, we can see the development of an increasingly abstract and capacious concept of political discourse, a concept built from figures that continued to point toward traditional oral forms.

Political writers found themselves making odd arguments when they used familiar local forms of talk to characterize an abstract arena, "the public," in which talk circulated. In many of these letters, the writers claim that clamor is both unanimous and divided; they claim to represent the "unanimous voice of the people" while disagreeing with "factious men." Others refer to coffeehouse talk that is both frivolous and so persuasive that it changes minds. The gaps and tensions between the claims these writers make and the figures they use to make them relate to what Michael Warner calls the "transpositions" central to a public sphere. A fully realized sphere of public opinion treats, for instance, ongoing discussion among groups of individuals as if it is deliberation leading to an articulated result—an opinion to which the state can respond. "Along the entire chain of equations in the public sphere—from local acts of reading or scenes of speech to a general horizon of public opinion and its critical opposition to state power—the pragmatics of public discourse must be systematically blocked from view."[2] The newspaper letters I will examine in this chapter reveal, in their tangled logic and multiple figures, the gaps and substitutions that make up this transposition. Rather than assuming the series of links Warner identifies, they display those links and the spaces between them, exposing the transposition between representations of particular conversations and a concept of "public discussion."

A writer in the *London Chronicle* of July 11, 1765, used clamor as a figure for circulating political opinion in an argument against the hugely unpopular Earl of Bute, the king's favorite and first minister. The letter chides the "individuals, who, from an affectation of superior understandings, pretend to think the clamour against the *Favourite* ill-founded, because they will not be of the same opinion with the vulgar." Unlike the clamors referred to by Jenkinson and Walpole in the previous chapter, which were circulated in privileged spaces by friends, this writer describes a phenomenon with the capacity to unite high and low social groups. The writer argues in favor of such unity: "let not these men of superior sagacity always determine to keep their eyes *shut*, because common people *see*." This formulation borrows the influential quality of clamor as we saw it deployed in the last chapter. When Lord Holland asked "every friend I have" to "help me in expressing" his gratitude, he could be assured that members of the faction currently in power would hear that expression at dinner and over cards in several different houses.[3] By using clamor as a figure to represent "what the common people see," rather than what influential people wish to express, the writer does more than mix print and aural metaphors. He suggests that his own letter is an important piece of evidence, part of a larger phenomenon to which important people ought to pay attention.

Many writers used the same figure with less positive connotations. Clamor was often characterized as evidence of division and dissatisfaction. Another letter, signed "A Moderate Man," distances itself from the sounds that the previous writer invites his readers to join: "popular clamour had long and loudly prevailed against the late administration, whether justly or not, I shall not here enquire; suffice it to say, his Majesty has been pleased to displace them and appoint others in their stead. . . ." The letter goes on to argue that the new ministers should be given some time to implement their policies, before being criticized.

In the *London Chronicle* for August 6, 1765, a satirical writer comments on the recent change in ministries by claiming that the following pamphlets have been published in France: "The Art of arriving to Riches and Honours, by despising the clamours of the People," and "A Change in Ministry stops the cries of the people without easing their wants." This writer imagines complaints in the form of pamphlets, demonstrating the linkage many writers made between printed objects and figurative language drawn from aural forms. Many writers explicitly referred to their own printed letters, and those of others, as parts of a larger "clamour" that could be figuratively "heard" everywhere. Clamor was already a metaphor when used in the courtly sense described in chapter 2: complaints heard over cards at one house, dinner at another, and in a confidential chat at a third were imagined as echoes of a single sound, rebounding from the many friends and supporters of a particular individual. In newspapers, this figure's associative chain was given further links. Clamor in a newspaper treats printed words, replicated by a machine, as echoes—they repeat and circulate. Like courtly clamor, these echoes indicate the influence and obligations of individuals bound in hierarchical relations of patronage.

As a figure, then, clamor in a newspaper links the exclusive world of a small political elite with a much larger and more heterogeneous group of newspaper readers. This linkage relates to a tension that has been noticed by many scholars of eighteenth-century press and politics. The institutional structure of politics, at midcentury, was still based around the court and the parliament. Voting was restricted to property holders, and nonexistent in the large industrial towns, where newspaper readers far outnumbered voters. Most members of Parliament felt that their role was not to represent or follow the wishes of their constituents but to make their own decisions about the questions before them. Within Parliament, groups of men with very similar political ideas jockeyed for power in the recurring pattern of "ins and outs" described in chapter 2.

How could the continuing influence of a small elite and "high" politics have coexisted with the many clamors, murmurs, and complaints from the "common people" reported in the newspaper passages I have quoted above? John Brewer and Kathleen Wilson, among others, have pointed out that despite this closed world of politics, "politicians and pamphleteers [frequently] spoke of . . . an all-embracing 'political nation'" of newspaper and pamphlet readers and coffeehouse habitués.[4]

Wilson has explored the extent of a "sense of the people" that was familiarly called upon by orators, newspaper writers, and pamphlets, as well as mobs and crowds.

Newspapers, especially those of the midcentury decades, explored these gaps and conflicts. In a period between wars, when changes of ministry were central political events, writers and readers worked to articulate their relationship to the negotiations among statesmen and courtiers. Charles E. Clark, discussing provincial papers in America, describes newspapers' address to their readers in terms of widened access to a privileged center, rather than a shift to a critical, empowered public: "by broadening access to current information and by dignifying in print the familiar concerns of everyday life, the newspapers offered a kind of open communion; ordinary readers were invited to share with a previously privileged circle in the ritual of communal identity in which one participated by reading the news."[5]

Historians' accounts of the gaps between popular ideologies of liberty and consent and state structures of hierarchy and exclusion form an interesting complement to work in public sphere theory, which has also focused on gaps between the concepts such as "public discussion" and any particular examples of public discussions. The tensions and gaps in contemporaries' accounts of the place of public opinion in their political system can be understood by looking at the way figurations piled up upon one another in the newspapers. By paying attention to writers' uses of courtly language to imagine political significance, I argue, we can see how contemporaries understood and negotiated the apparent conflict between the midcentury's vibrant popular political culture and that culture's practical separation from political structures.[6]

For an example of how individual political writers represented public opinion through figures of echoing sounds, we will now turn to a letter to the printer published in the *London Chronicle* for July 23, 1765. This letter provides an example of amplification. It represents public opinion in terms of echoing sounds, either unhappy clamor or happy acclaim. This letter, like many that year, ascribes the nation's problems to the "secret influence" of John Stuart, the third Earl of Bute. Bute had been George III's tutor before his accession to the throne in 1760, and he remained a close friend of the king. In May 1762, the king had appointed Bute first lord of the treasury, just in time for him to take the blame for the enormously unpopular Peace of Paris, which ended the Seven Years' War with concessions to France that many English people considered to be too large.

Bute's unpopularity increased as the year went on, as newspaper writers and members of the government compared him unfavorably with his highly popular predecessor William Pitt (the Elder). Bute was finally forced, partly by the strength of public opinion, to resign in April 1763. He was succeeded by George Grenville. Many people in England, however, concluded that Bute was still ruling in secret, or "behind the curtain." These rumors survived two more short-lived administrations; anyone in office was in danger of being seen as the tool of Lord Bute.

This letter comments on a new ministry being created by Cumberland, Newcastle, and Rockingham to take the place of Grenville's. It begins with a description of the day three years earlier when Bute had brought the Peace of Paris to Parliament for its approval (Parliament approved the treaty by a large margin, despite its unpopularity with many in the "political nation"). The letter does not make an abstract or explicitly theoretical argument. Instead it tells a story about an exchange between Bute (called "A Certain Nobleman" to get around the libel laws) and an ordinary Londoner:

> To the Printer.
>
> The day a certain Nobleman's Peace was to be laid formally before the Legislature for their approbation, though he was sufficiently secure of that, jealousy of conscience filled him with such fears of the people, that he had the whole way he was to go lined with a set of fellows, who, under the appearance of loitering to see the sight, should be ready to defend him from present insult or danger. But high as the resentment of the people was, it had not so far got the better of their respect to the laws, as to break out into violence; and they contented themselves with giving it vent in hisses and execrations, of which latter, one of the meanest of the mob was so liberal, echoing his name with the most horrid curses tagged to it in his very ear, as he passed by, that his myrmidons, to shew their vigilance, dogged him out of the crowd, and seizing him when separated from his companions, dragged him away to the minister, who was just then returned home in triumph.
>
> When he was brought into his presence, for he would see him himself, to try if he could, either by threats or promises, prevail upon him to own who had set him on, as the meanness of his appearance made it improbable, that he should otherwise concern himself about matters so much above him: his Lordship, on hearing his offence, asked him what injury he had ever done him? to which the fellow answered, "None."—"For what reason then," said he sternly, "did you curse me in that insolent and outrageous manner?" "I don't know," answered the fellow, "I did it, because I hear every body do so wherever I go: that was all my reason."

Struck with a reply, that shewed the general sense of the people in so strong a light, he had scarce spirit to order the fellow to be dismissed, nor from that time was heard a shout in the street, that did not make his heart quake within him; till his terrors at length raised so high, that he shrunk behind the scene for shelter, and resigned all outward appearance of power to substitutes, who undertook to execute his orders and bear the brunt, till the storm should be laid.

To silence and subdue the spirit of this resentment, for it was equally contrary to his disposition and designs to remove it by changing his measures; methods were pursued utterly inconsistent with the spirit of the laws of the land; and which would have reduced the liberty of the subject to a mere name, had not some of the dispensers of those laws supported them with a firmness and integrity worthy of their sacred charge.

For the pursuit of such schemes, the honour and interest of the nation were so shamefully neglected, in every instance, foreign and domestic, and the minds of the people filled with such discontent and jealousy of their Governors, that prudent apprehension trembled to look forward, struck with the consequences which had followed a similar conduct in the reign of James the First; with this difference indeed, that in that case the cause proceeded entirely from himself; whereas, in the present, it arose solely from a minister, and is removed by his removal from power; as there can be no just reason to fear, that his successors should follow measures, their spirited and just opposition to which, raised them to the confidence of their Sovereign, and the good opinion of their fellow subjects; without the support of which, so recent an instance must convince them, that no power can be permanent among a free people: which removal is an act so gracious in the Prince, and so grateful to his faithful people, that it has entirely dispersed all those clouds which had for some time overcast their happiness, and restored voice to that love which echoed his every step at the commencement of his reign, and is the only sure foundation of his own and his family's greatness and glory.

A. Marvel

Sound is central to this piece. The people "give [their resentment] vent in hisses and execrations. . . ." Their love for George III is also a sound. He has "restored voice to that love which echoed his every step at the commencement of his reign. . . ." This phrase represents a literal, not a figurative, "voice of the people." George III, the first Hanoverian monarch who spoke English and considered himself British, was greeted at his coronation and wedding with bonfires and cheering crowds wherever he went. Those crowds and the sound of their cheering are here called up to describe the people's loyalty. The people's sentiments, both their love for the king and their hatred for Bute, "echo" from person to person. Bute responds to the crowd's feelings as sound by desiring "to silence and subdue the spirit of this resentment." Public opinion, then, is represented as sound. And the purpose of the story this piece tells is to show how very widespread that sound is. The "meanest of the mob" reflects the nature of this sound by "echoing [Bute's] name with the most horrid curses tagged to it."

In describing the people's responses to the various changes in administration, this writer creates an image in print of a sound that echoes so much that it can be heard not just in every drawing room in the West End, but in every street, "wherever I go," as the "mean man" says. The writer, who signs himself "A. Marvel" (suggesting both that the story he tells is marvelous and that he sympathizes with the republicanism of Andrew Marvell), works to make a strong case for the political importance of the "echoing voice" he describes. Like clamor in court circles, this phenomenon involves requests from less powerful people to the king (remove Bute and give his job to someone we can trust) and like clamor in court circles, this is a request made in the form of echoing sound. Unlike the clamor heard at supper tables in the West End, however, this sound is not motivated by personal ambition, or by anything at all. The sound is perpetuated by other sounds: "I did it," the mean man explains, "because I hear every body do so wherever I go: that was all my reason." The man's ignorance and thoughtlessness are virtuous because they show that he is not motivated by the desire for patronage. His curses are not the clamor of a particular court faction, but rather they show "the general sense of the people."

The twenty-first-century reader might expect Bute to react with scorn to a member of a mob who does not know why he holds the views he makes so much noise about. Instead, Bute reacts with terror. The writer makes it clear that Bute knew from beginning of the story that there would be a mob. Ahead of time, he had hired goons to defend him. But he is represented as thinking of this mob as a traditional English one, "raised" by its social superiors through a combination of money, free beer, and the emotional resonance of traditional English values. Thus he asks the man "who had set him on, as the meanness of his appearance made it improbable, that he should otherwise concern himself about matters so much above him." Bute is afraid when he realizes that this man has not been "set on"; he reflects a general, popular opinion, rather than the usual opposition of a rival court party. One of the writer's main claims in this piece is that Bute and all other ministers are, and should continue to be, afraid of such popular clamor.

The last paragraph tells newspaper readers what they should watch for in the acts of the new administration and the king, and it is a warning to the administration and the king that the people are watching and ready to erupt into clamorous gratefulness or complaint. The writer makes these claims in a long and tortuous sentence:

> . . . as there can be no just reason to fear, that [Grenville's] successors [in the new administration] should follow measures, their spirited and just opposition to which, raised them to the confidence of their Sovereign, and the good opinion of their fellow subjects; without the support of which, so recent an instance must convince them, that no power can be permanent among a free people: which removal is an act so gracious in the Prince, and so grateful to his faithful people, that it has entirely dispersed all those clouds which had for some time overcast their happiness, and restored voice to that love which echoed his steps at the commencement of his reign, and is the only sure foundation of his own and his family's greatness and glory.

The repeated links made with the word "which" help this writer to construct a very complex and delicately balanced chain of cause and effect. Because Grenville's successors opposed his measures, they will not employ such measures themselves. They hold their positions because they have popular support, but only because the king was attentive to that popular support. The people rely on the king to follow their wishes, but his glory rests upon doing so. Thus the writer claims that nothing can possibly go wrong in the new administration and at the same time warns it to watch its step. This kind of self-contradictory and anxious claim is characteristic of newspaper letters during this decade, which frequently argue that the people cannot be fooled but should be vigilant or that they are united but divided.

The challenge this writer faces is to make a credible claim for the importance of the "general sense of the people" in the day-to-day working of the government. He claims that the new ministers were appointed by "the confidence of their Sovereign, and the good opinion of their fellow subjects." Historians, and the diaries and letters of the people who made up this new ministry, however, show that while public distrust of the old one had to do with its disintegration, the new one was patched together through the usual process of factional negotiation and deal making.[7]

To imaginatively compass these contradictions, this writer represents the common people as extensions of the court world. They provide a further series of spaces in which sounds can echo, moving up from clients to patrons and eventually to the king. These conversations are not imagined as part of a town separate from the court. Instead, the town here is an extension of the court. This is a unanimity that has two modes: clamor and acclaim.

In both clamor and acclaim, reasoned argument or deliberation would be a handicap, since they would dilute the unanimity, as well as probably the volume, of the sound. The mean man's comment that "I did it, because I hear every body do so wherever I go: that was all my reason," is very far from the kind of discourse Jürgen Habermas describes, in which "the authority of the better argument could . . . carry the day." The mean man does not have the best argument; he has no argument at all. He has a shared feeling, which he expresses in sound, further echoing the sounds already circulating around him. Those sounds are familiar and recognizable, made as part of the politics of patronage and loyalty stretching back into the English past. The difference, which confuses and frightens Bute in this passage, is that the sounds have multiplied. They have gone beyond the clamor traditionally available for being "called up" by an influential figure. In this way, the urban crowd depicted in the piece, larger and more anonymous than a group of rioters in a country town or suburban neighborhood, is similar to the newspaper's audience, a widespread group among whom discourse circulates. The newspaper's circulation, its "public," is comprehensible through a metaphorical link to a familiar form of circulating discourse: courtly clamor becomes popular clamor.

The new ministers are given two choices in this piece: they can hear applause or clamor. These images do not represent discussion as a process of examining and refining ideas; they represent talk as the expression of opinions. These opinions are described as inevitable reactions to indisputable truths. A letter published in the *Public Advertiser* on April 24, 1774, made the same point: "there is still Virtue and Vigor enough left in the British Heart to follow the Protector of the Honour and Dignity of his Country with well-directed Applause, and to mark with infamy and Disgrace the Betrayer of its legal Rights and Interests." This writer is an opponent of the American colonists' arguments about representation, and thus we could read him as conservative. The letter begins, however, with an argument in favor of opening the doors of the House of Lords to the public and the press. It is because the public can engage in applause or "marking [bad representatives] with infamy," according to this writer, that publishing details of the debates will have positive effects.

As clamor becomes a figure of a figure—a print representation of a series of sounds figured as an echo—it gains a quality of abstraction equivalent to modern social concepts such as nation, class, and society. But it does not represent several other qualities usually associated with newspaper presentations of public opinion in this period—rational critique, economic self-interest, discussion. Clamor does not suggest conversational *exchange.* "The people," when they clamor, do not address each other. Instead, they address the state, which either responds to the sound or does not. This writer, in finding a powerful image for the political participation of his readers, imagines them like broadsides, saying the same single thing over and over everywhere they go. Clamor does not provide an image for the people addressing each other; nor does it provide an image of a newspaper writer addressing the people.

We can see some crucial differences between a public imagined through ongoing debate and a public imagined through amplified clamor by examining newspaper writers who disagreed with A. Marvel. These writers criticize, not the positions A. Marvel takes on the peace treaty, but his positive characterizations of clamor and applause as media for popular participation in politics. For them, the alternative to clamor is not applause but silence. According to these writers, when the people have no cause for complaint, there is nothing to be said. Unlike a Habermasian public sphere, which measures its own vitality through ongoing debate, the polity these writers describe cycles back and forth from unhappy clamor to satisfied silence.

Defending the new ministry, a letter signed "Indolens," which appeared in the *London Evening Post* for August 1, 1765, wished for silence:

> . . . under a Ministry so popular as the present, chosen out from amongst the favourites of the people, by the most amiable of Monarchs, with the assistance of a great Prince, whose whole life has been one continued series of patriotism, I am almost ready to indulge the flattering hope that popular clamour and party spirit will subside; but when I reflect upon the fluctuating temper of my countrymen, and their readiness to take fire at the instigations of every artful Writer, who can skillfully employ the pen to blacken characters, and misrepresent the conduct of those who preside at the helm—this calm seems but the forerunner of destructive storms.

The writer predicts pessimistically that "complaints and murmurs will begin to arise, hireling Writers will start up, those who are now in disgrace will begin to shake off despair, and all will be as it ever has been, except in the few years of Mr. Pitt's Administration." This writer uses clamor as a figure for mixing media; clamor subsides until artful writers employ their pens, and hireling writers are started up by complaints and murmurs. The happy state this writer wishes for would be calm—no clamor, no party spirit, no complaints and murmurs. The Latin "indolens" suggests here the absence of pain, as well as the English sense of the lack of work there would be for political writers in such a quiet situation.

The fact that Indolens *is* a political writer, of course, raises a difficult question. If clamor and party spirit are symptoms of national political ill health, why contribute? This letter is a response to others, created by "hireling Writers" on the side of ministers who would not serve the country best. Indolens implies in this way that he is not a hireling and is participating in the noise only because otherwise it would be dominated by self-interested noisemakers.

Many political letter writers shared this sense that clamor could be "heard," figuratively, in the newspapers, and that virtuous action on the part of state and people would reduce it to silence. A letter published in the *London Evening-Post* August 1, 1765, gives a method for discovering whether political letters have been written by hirelings. "It is no difficult matter to discern the motives of those who condemn an Administration, or to distinguish the difference between men, who write out of principle, and for the good of their country, and those who write out of prejudice, or for their private interests, *by their own writings*." Calumny characterizes the latter, he argues. "Such men will fall open-mouth'd upon a Ministry, and call them all the hard names they can think of, before they are half-formed, or have had time to take any measures at all, either good or bad." The clamors one might hear at Bedford house or at a club frequented by the Grenvilles and Temples are, in this letter, amplified by appearing in print. Rather than circulating among the friends and allies of the old ministers, the "hard names" are written in the papers. Readers far out of the circles of high politics can observe the spectacle of men angrily clamoring against each others' actions.

Like Indolens, this writer sees such written noise as a sign of political problems and wishes it away: "the Public, therefore, will beware of such men, and when they hear them loudly clamouring against a ministry, before they have had an opportunity of acting, or shewing their intentions, they will despise them; as knowing they do not make such clamour for their good or interest, but for their own private views and advantages." This writer characterizes his opponents as writing for their private advantage and advises the public to despise them, suggesting that like clamor, public and private are familiar concepts that do not need to be defined or defended. The public he addresses is constituted through its ability to be suspicious of the clamor and keep quiet, rather than through its participation. In this way, the letter recognizes the legitimacy of a public constituted through access to clamor. Newspaper readers are, figuratively, within earshot and thus part of the ongoing circulating discourse of the political nation.

Even writers dismissive of popular political participation imagined a wide public "hearing" the "noise" made by day-to-day politics. Such a writer commented in the *London Chronicle* for December 15, 1772, "I hear the tools of discontent by turns declaim, see ejected Statesmen anxious to regain the places they have lost, and hear mobs halloo, inspired by men of much better heads, but much worse bosoms than themselves. These noisy chiefs of mighty factions, just appear to me like women struggling for precedence, or full grown boys for toys and trifles." The letter ends with the comment that "one Cincinnatus is of more real value than all the noisy Babblers which disturb the peace of Britain." Like Indolens, this writer claims to wish only for silence, which is equated with peace. But all three of these writers themselves plunge into the fray; all assume that a public is constituted by the noise itself, and imagine that peace is to be secured only by that public's ability to restrain itself from joining the "halloo."

All the letters examined in this chapter agree in imagining the political nation as constituted through the figurative echoes of clamor. Such figures allowed writers and readers to name and shape the flow of political discourse circulating around them. These figures do not, however, necessarily provide an empirical description of how newspapers were produced and distributed. For all their distaste for "hireling writers," for instance, several of the writers above were probably precisely that. Their fulsome praise for particular factions ("a Ministry so popular as the present, chosen out from amongst the favourites of the people") suggests affiliation, if not dependence. Until recently, press historians have seen eighteenth-century newspapers as almost entirely controlled by subsidies from the various "ins and outs" in high politics. More recent work on newspaper finances has demonstrated papers depended primarily on advertising revenue, but they did receive assistance (or bribes, or subsidies) from individuals and from the secret service throughout the century.[8] Writers hired by parties also sent "letters to the printer." The Earl of Sandwich, for instance, hired a clergyman named James Scott to write letters supporting him and the Grenvilles. Scott was one of the more successful such writers, according to Robert Rea:

> About 1764, Scott became intimate with Sandwich, Halifax, and other members of Grenville's ministry, and under their patronage he wrote the series of letters signed 'Anti-Sejanus,' which appeared in the Public Advertiser. Scott possessed more than moderate ability, and Anti-Sejanus was one of the most popular writers of short articles between Wilkes and Junius. He hewed to the party line, attacked 'the favorite' as well as the Rockingham Whigs, and maintained a high regard for George Grenville. It has been said that Scottt's letters were so popular that the sale of the Public Advertiser was increased from 1,500 to 3,000 daily. Scott's Anti-Sejanus letters drew replies from 'An Occasional Writer' for the Rockingham ministry in 1765, and John Almon believed that Edmund Burke, among others, wrote several replies to Scott. Grenville's use of 'every coffee-house and every newspaper' to sway opinion enabled Scott to retire in 1771, unbowed and undefeated.[9]

The letters written by "Junius" in 1769 were a sensation, boosting sales, electrifying politics, and leading to several trials and an interest in tracking down the writer's identity that motivated amateur sleuths well into the nineteenth century. In each of these cases, the letters were written and published as part of the traditional and familiar strategy of "creating a clamour" described in chapter 2. It is important to note that such letters did not dominate newspapers, however. They appeared among paragraphs of news, advertisements, reviews of plays and books, verse, and discussions of manners, history, geography, and shipping.

Like the images used in the letters themselves, the information we have about the production of newspapers suggest that a wider public was being invited in to the circle of high politics. Through figurations such as clamor, writers explained the significance of media in politics. Writers hired by factions, when they referred to clamor, were doing the same thing they had always done, but they were increasing each echo's repetitions by having their complaints appear in multiple copies of a daily paper.

These letters represent an ongoing series of claims and counterclaims made for and about a general, anonymous audience that supported or opposed particular people and policies associated with the day-to-day functioning of the state. Today we might refer to such a phenomenon as public discussion or debate. Those terms are absent from the letters we have looked at so far, and from many others that claim to represent political talk. How is clamor related to public discussion or debate? For Habermas, the central issue in debate is authority, or legitimacy. The conceptual change that interests him has to do with the source of legitimacy: does it derive from traditional social forms, such as aristocracy, church, and state? Or does it derive from rational analysis of evidence? The newspaper letters we have been looking at suggest that there is another possible source of legitimacy: the unanimous sentiments of the people. The importance of this concept in eighteenth-century England has been excellently documented by Kathleen Wilson in her book *The Sense of the People*. Like the newspaper writers quoted in this chapter, Wilson believes that many English people understood a "sense" of national loyalty shared and expressed by common people as an important political force. It is important to note, however, that Wilson's title is singular: the people, as a unit, have a singular sense, rather than a series of arguments or a process of discussion.

Rather than through the use of the terms "discussion" or "debate," midcentury newspaper writers negotiated differences of opinion and interest by juxtaposing figures of echoing, repeated, circulating sound. Different accounts of clamor were presented in adjacent columns; figures of clamor were juxtaposed with figures of coffeehouse chat. It is this juxtaposition, as we will see, that creates the effect of an accessible, open, public sphere where rank and personal attachment are irrelevant.

Like clamor, coffeehouse chat frequently found its way into newspapers. Overheard conversations, allegorical speakers, and wandering urban observers populated newspaper columns. Political essays often began by setting up familiar scenes of tavern or coffeehouse conversation: "Some members of our Tory Club in Wiltshire, benighted after a long Fox Chace, took Refuge lately in a Public House, where we drank hard, and talked much Politics."[10] By juxtaposing *Spectator*-like scenes of political talk with clamorous figures, newspapers represented differences of opinion and interest that their writers did not name as debates or discussions. Coffeehouse talk, clamor, and conversation are so juxtaposed in a letter that appeared in the *London Chronicle* for July 9, 1765. It was clear in early July that yet another change in administration was underway. Speculation was rampant. The letter writer, signing himself "Veritas," described the climate:

> Manifesto's begin to appear; parties are preparing for a paper-war; and little doubt can be entertained of there being, for at least some time to come, abundant matter for Coffee-house controversies, and family conversation.
>
> The Champions of either side are trumpeting their own respective merits and praises, and at the same time depreciating the pretensions of their adversaries. But as doubtless all have high pretensions, in their own opinions at least, and may flatter themselves with believing the public can be easily persuaded to have the same, it may perhaps be as much an act of kindness to them as of justice to the people, to signify to all what the present opinions of the public are with respect to them.

Although he does refer to "controversies," Veritas does not set up his piece as part of a debate or refer to the public as engaged in discussion. Instead, like the writers quoted above, he deprecates the "trumpeting" originating from the Grenvilles, Rockinghams, and other groupings attempting to control the distribution of places in the new ministry.

Veritas makes the people's conversations and controversies dependent upon and secondary to actions of the ministry. The "matter" upon which these conversations are based is the manifestos put out by the two sides in the paper war. The substance comes from these suspect sources, and the conversations can only comment on it. A similar account had been published early in January of the same year by a writer signing T.B., who complained that Parliament had been out of session for too long. It was terrible, he wrote, "to see two winter months pass over, and not one vote of the house of commons to descant upon in the course of a long tedious evening. It looks like a chasm in government, or a kind of interregnum."[11] The language in which the public's political interest is described here suggests both orality and frivolity. The word "descant" comes originally from music, indicating, according to the *OED,* "a melodious accompaniment to a simple musical theme . . . often merely extemporized, above it. . . ." As early as the sixteenth century, the word had also been used to indicate "varied comment on a theme, amplification of a subject; a comment, criticism, observation, remark." Using the word "descant" to describe political talk suggests that such talk is decorative, like music, another way of filling long winter evenings. The activity of substance, in this image, comes from Parliament. The voice or voices of the people embellish it.

For both Veritas and T.B., the public's political talk is dependent upon and derivative of the work done in government, which provides the matter. T.B. hopes that "the beginning of the year sixty-five will afford a more plentiful crop of political chat, than the barren close of sixty-four." Veritas's letter attempts to claim that such chat is both vitally important to the nation and idle and frivolous, both unified and divided. The center of his piece is a list of "the opinions of the public" about the parties who are in competition for places:

> The bo-peep Vizier [Bute] is so generally detested, that it is most ardently wished the fullest security was had of his being never in a situation to touch the helm more.
>
> Mr. Pitt, on the contrary, is so generally respected, and possesses so entirely the confidence of the public, that it is eagerly desired he should be permitted to guide.
>
> Those who are going out, are bid heartily farewell: and the public take leave of them . . . with wishing they may never again see their faces at court; where they have condescended to act the parts of Mock-Statesmen, and be the most abject instruments of one [Bute] who himself durst not appear to lead, . . .
>
> Those who are coming in, are not feared, but they are doubted; and therefore it will behove them, by their conduct, to establish their credit. The continuation of a certain influence [Bute's] is greatly dreaded, from the ill success of some late negotiations; and if they suffer themselves to be made cyphers in office, they will become blots in popularity. . . . The present critical situation of affairs makes it needful for a soul of great policy to shine forth in new and great plans, to be executed with assiduity; and these must likewise honestly appear in measures for essentially restoring and invigorating our constitution, as also for removing jealousies, and restoring harmony among the people.

All the men Veritas names are "so generally detested" or "so generally respected" that a reporting of these facts seems almost unnecessary. The whole passage is written in the passive voice, suggesting, as the reference to coffeehouse conversation does, that the public is reactive and frivolous rather than active and important. Veritas complicates things still further by claiming that one of the jobs of the new administration will be "removing jealousies, and restoring harmony among the people." If the people's opinions are as general, and as "hearty" as he has described them be, what could be the nature of this jealousy and inharmoniousness? The conversations in coffeehouses and families are provoked by these trumpetings and manifestos. Rather than engaging in such noise, he proposes instead to "signify to all" a unified message explaining clearly "the present opinions of the public." Unity and division are tricky issues for a writer with such a plan; if the sense of the people is a legitimate political force only when it is unified, then a political writer can find himself explaining "the public" to "all."

Veritas claims that the origin of any jealousies or differences among the people would have to be the insinuations and manipulations of would-be officeholders around the court. The ideas he has described "are unquestionably the present opinions of parties and persons. Whoever believe otherwise are deceivers of themselves: and whoever at this time attempt to make the people think otherwise, will fail in their endeavors, and of course labor in vain." As with the earlier part of the letter, where Veritas claimed to be explaining the ideas of "all" to "the public," he here makes a confusing group of distinctions. "Parties, "persons," and "the people" all think in the way he has described. But there are also these "whoevers," who might believe otherwise or try to make the people believe otherwise. His vagueness is both legal and formal—he does not want to accuse anyone in particular of venality and so risk legal action for libel. But it is also a productive vagueness. By juxtaposing "any," "all," "whoever," "conversation," "controversy," "harmony," and "trumpetings," Veritas indicates a condition of ongoing circulating discourse while claiming to represent only a healthy, optimistic, and unified sense of the people. Piling up multiple aural figures allows this writer to gesture toward an abstraction we might identify as a "public sphere" without questioning the legitimacy of traditional ways of doing politics.

A poem printed in the *Public Advertiser* on May 6 of the same year provides an example of how juxtaposed figures and media can indicate a condition of public political talk that individual writers do not name or represent. The poem evokes an abstract world of circulating political discourse while arguing in favor of silence and the status quo. In it, we can see how the figures we have been examining could enable political imagination despite their connection to traditional concepts and conservative arguments. The poem was probably written by a dependent of a particular court figure, attempting to argue in favor of his patron's concept of good government and to quiet criticism of his policies. By juxtaposing figures of popular political discourse, however, the poet evokes the circulating, abstract condition of the popular political talk he is attempting to silence:

To *any* Minister or great Man.

Whether you lead the Patriot Band,
Or in the Class of Courtiers stand,
Or prudently prefer
The middle Course, with equal Zeal
To serve both King and Common-weal,
Your Grace, my Lord, or Sir!

Know, Minister! whate'er your Plan,
Whate'er your Politics, great Man!
You must expect Detraction;
Though of clean Hand and honest Heart,
Your Greatness must expect to smart
Beneath the Rod of Faction.

Like Blockheads, eager in Dispute,
The Mob, that many-headed Brute,
All bark and bawl together,
For Continental Measures some,
And some cry, Keep your Troops at home,
And some are pleased with neither.

Lo! a Militia guards the Land;
Thousands applaud your saving Hand,
And hail you their Protector;
While Thousands censure and defame,
And brand you with the hideous Name
of State-Quack or Projector.

Are active, vig'rous Means preferr'd?
Lord! what Harangues are hourly heard
Of wasted Blood and Treasure!
Then all for Enterprize and Plot,
And, Pox o'this unmeaning Scot!
If cautious be your Measure.

Corruption's Influence you despise;
These lift your Glory to the Skies;
Those pluck your Glory down;
So strangely diff'rent is the Note
Of Scoundrels that have Right to vote,
And Scoundrels that have none.

Ye then who guide the Car of State,
Scorning the Rabble's idle Prate,
Proceed as ye design'd;
In rugged Ways, the Reins and Steeds
Alone the skilful Driver heeds,
Nor stays to cut behind.

The mob's noise, in this poem, is produced by conflict between opposed loyalties. The poet begins by calling all "detraction" the effect of the "rod of faction." This suggests that the criticism ministers receive is all the result of divisions created by rivals for power. In the next stanza, the poet begins a series of paired oppositions that structures the rest of the poem. Some people are for sending troops to the continent, some for keeping them at home. Some are promilitia; some think the militia is a strange innovation. Some support prosecuting war vigorously, others against risking the money and lives.

The interactions between these opposing views, however, are not called a debate. Instead, the writer mentions barking, brawling, a cry, applause, hailing, and "Harangues" "hourly heard." People who disagree about corruption have different "notes." All of these noises are summed up in the final stanza as "Prate," a form of prattle or inconsequential talk. These oral terms are used to indicate the mob cannot resolve disputes through discussions. The people bark and brawl, but they do so "together." The mob is a singular brute with many heads. If the people were reasoning individuals, or even members of competing interest groups, it would be understandable that they had differing ideas. If they are a single unit, the mob, then their opposed ideas are just senseless noise. Because there is no unified "sense of the people," in this view, there is no political meaning.

The odd and contradictory thing about this poem is that it pays so much attention to a phenomenon that it encourages its addressee to ignore. The speaker claims that the mob is bestial and factious, and that its sound is inarticulate. Yet he shows an awareness of the issues that spurred the most political discussion at the time: relations with France and Spain, militias versus standing armies, imperialism and national honor, corruption, and the franchise. The speaker claims that the talk of the mob or the rabble is irrelevant but spends seven stanzas describing it. The poem argues that the talk is incomprehensible, yet addresses its major concerns specifically. It claims repeatedly that the sounds of the mob are meaningless, but yet it is able to list the issues important to newspaper writers and readers at the time.

The poem's speaker disowns any specific political ideas whatsoever. By addressing the poem to any minister or great man, the speaker endorses any and all measures that look good from a position in the driver's seat of state. But the poem is a seven-stanza comment on the speaker's refusal to take a position in politics.

What does it mean to publish a poem like this in a newspaper? Because the newspaper was sold cheaply and widely, its audience was not the one addressed rhetorically by this poem's speaker. The addressee is a great man, presumably above the speaker. In addressing itself to a single ear positioned above its own speaker in a hierarchy, the poem takes the form of clamor. But rather than being spoken by many people for an audience of one, this poem was printed. It was published for reading by a large, anonymous audience, an audience interested precisely in the issues that this poet claims it cannot understand. It is "the mob" and "the rabble" who will read this poem, as well as perhaps a great man or someone he pays to keep tabs on the newspapers.

There are many ways in which this poem is distinctively a printed text. The author is anonymous; the descriptions are generalized. The poem is not quite a prediction and not quite a description of what has happened in the past. Instead it creates an ongoing present in which certain kinds of things happen. Like other pieces we have looked at, this writer makes a claim: "this is the way things are today." Benedict Anderson and Jürgen Habermas have suggested that print made such generality both easier to imagine and easier to represent. It would be possible to see this poem as an example of a writer valorizing print by attacking orality, except that there is no purpose for print in this vision of politics. The speaker does not argue that the public should read more carefully, be more rational, make more careful use of information, or make better arguments. The poem argues that the public should be ignored. If the speaker disapproves of political noise, he is equally disapproving of political print.

A poem full of discordant noises and tense issues argues for silence and for solitary decision making. A newspaper piece makes an argument that the paper's readers should be ignored. This poem is an example of the productive power of juxtaposed figurations in newspaper writing. The writer does not imagine the paper's readers engaged, even as spectators, in the sort of "public use of reason" Kant would describe nineteen years later as the central activity of a reading public. But the poem does figure circulating discourse and name it as a general phenomenon. It participates in a condition of discourse that it represents as impossible. The figures of factional sound—applause, cries, prattle—

remove the argument from a particular scene and suggest, in their layered significations, an abstract concept of ongoing political conversation. This poem does not represent Habermas's public sphere, or Kant's, because its participants do not recognize rationality or seek the general good. But it does represent an abstract public constituted through circulating discourse.

None of the newspaper pieces discussed so far in this chapter represents the specifics of the conversations to which it refers. Instead, they characterize and generalize those conversations—as clamor, coffeehouse talk, or applause. Turning to a piece that does represent political dialogue, we will see that the dynamic of using juxtaposed figures to imagine an arena of circulating discourse is active here as well. Using the *Spectator*'s familiar convention of recording talk overheard in a coffeehouse, this writer renders a particular political discussion as part of a circulating mass of talk that is important as a figure of the times. The letter, which appeared in the *Public Advertiser* on July 18, 1770, is signed "Moderator:"

> Sir,
>
> Looking over a Volume of Swift the other Day, I met with the following Passage: When somebody was telling a certain great Minister that the People were discontented, 'Poh, said he, half a Dozen Fools are prating in a Coffee-house, and presently imagine their own Noise about their Ears is made by the World;' than which nothing can, in my Opinion, be more applicable to the present noisy and insignificant Race of Patriots. In order, however, to convey to your Readers a more lively Idea of these Ideots, I shall endeavour to amuse them with a Conversation, or rather Dispute, which I accidentally overheard between two Persons at a Coffee-house in this Metropolis, a Scotchman and an Hibernian.
>
> SCOT. Well, Sir, I hope you entertain a more favourable Opinion of the Measures of Government than at our last Meeting.
>
> HIB. No, Sir; nor shall I while there are such a set of S— —ls at the Head of Affairs.
>
> SCOT. Be not so vociferous, Sir. Cannot you reason coolly upon the subject?
>
> HIB. How the Devil should a Man reason coolly, as you call it, when he is provoked!
>
> SCOT. But if you will give me Leave, I will endeavor to convince you.
>
> HIB. Convice me! Do you think that you or any Man can convince me I'm in the wrong, when I know myself to be in the right? Why is our Navy so totally neglected? For what are so many Reviews? Why to cut your Heads off to be sure [Here a loud Laugh by the Company.]

SCOT. My dear Sir, your Patriotism seems to get the better of your Understanding. Your reasoning is vague and undecisive.

HIB. [Striding across the Room]. Don't tell me, Sir, my Reasoning is like that of an honest Man.—I'm a Friend to the Revolution; I'm a Friend to the Family upon the Throne, and I'm a Friend to K.G. as long as he's a Friend to his People, and no longer by G-d.

SCOT. Do you know where you are, Sir, that you talk in this Manner?

HIB. Yes, Sir, I am in a public Coffee-Room; I speak my Sentiments, and will maintain them to the last Drop of my Blood.

> Such, Mr. Woodfall, was the Language of this Liberty Boy, whose Stupidity, like to that of most of his Brethren, served as an effectual Bulwark to his Designs. I must confess my Choler was at one Time so far raised, that I could hardly suppress my Indignation; thinking him, however, unworthy of my Notice, and that there was no great Danger of his gaining many Proselytes in his Favour, I sauntered out of the Coffee-house.

Like the pieces discussed above, this one argues that particular kinds of discourse do not reveal the sense of the people but only the complaints of a faction discontented to be out of office. The "present race of patriots" refers to the opposition, particularly the Wilkite City element. Like the poem, this dialogue is written in favor of the ministry in power, in this case Lord North's. Neither piece attempts to represent a debate or evaluate evidence. Like the poem, this dialogue characterizes political discourse itself as a sign of political decay. Irrationality is attributed to the Hibernian, who claims that it would be impossible to convince him to change his views, because he knows himself to be in the right. But the piece as a whole takes a similar view of political conversation, suggesting that talk is either irrelevant or pernicious.

The writer represents the Hibernian's words as clamor—he is being carried away by his patriotism, or support for the opposition. More characterizations of political speech produce more layers of signification and thus of abstraction. This dialogue layers opposition clamor, coffeehouse chat, and allegorical Scotch and Irish men. It makes several references to the conventions of coffeehouse chat: the passage from Swift explicitly calls upon the era of Addison and Steele. The Hibernian points out that "I am in a public coffee room" as a defense of his speech. The allegorical Scotchman and Hibernian represent people meddling in what is above them. As colonial subjects of Britain, and as anonymous coffeehouse habitués, they have views on military policy only because they need something to fill their time. Thus they are in the tradition of "Abraham Froth" and his clubmates described in *Spectator* no. 43.

Using dialogue form allows the poet to spread out the sounds that the poem above represents the mob as making "together." By separating those sounds into a dialogue, the writer gives even more attention to the specifics of the sounds he denigrates. By piling on layers of signification, writers imply a further abstraction, a realm "imagined" in Benedict Anderson's terms, or "fictive" in Michael Warner's, where ongoing political discussions produce public opinion. Clamor, as a term for political talk, refers to any particular speech or piece of writing as part of a larger phenomenon in which a message is repeated in different spaces. The meaning of the single utterance is determined by its relation to many others and to the spaces and institutions surrounding them. The term clamor, then, abstracts; it relates something particular to something general. Juxtaposing such abstractions, as these writers do when they characterize the political situation by listing clamor, chat, prattle, applause, and cries, creates a second-order abstraction. Each of these terms refers to a space, an institution, a way of speaking: a figurative public. By juxtaposing coffeehouse and courtly publics, writers gesture toward a concept of circulating discourse abstracted even from particular rooms and particular habits of speech. A conceptual space where such figurative publics themselves interact is similar to the public sphere Habermas describes, in which the particular histories and preferences of the participants in a discussion are subordinated to the act of discussion itself. These writers do not name such a concept, however, or refer to it familiarly. Instead, they signify its possibility by layering figures of more local and traditional publics.

The Scot begins the conversation by hoping for "a more favourable opinion of the Measures of Government." He is looking for support for North's administration, and in this way, his speech is connected to party politics. He is inviting his friend to participate in applause, the positive complement of clamor. But by layering applause, coffeehouse chat, and clamor with an allegorical dialogue, this writer is forced to characterize the speech of the position he endorses, as well as the one he denigrates. As a result, the Scotchman mentions reason, precision, and moderation and uses a modest and polite tone. A dialogue between two such speakers would be quite different from any of the pieces we have seen so far in this chapter: more rational, more abstract, quieter. When they characterized political talk, figuring it as public, midcentury newspaper writers indicated the possibility of such rational, unaffiliated political discussion only negatively, as an abstraction of all the various, loud, familiar sounds they named.

In his definition of the public sphere, Kant uses a similar strategy for naming the realm of enlightenment. "For this enlightenment, nothing is required but freedom . . . But I hear from all sides the cry: Do not argue! The officer says: Do not argue but drill! The tax official: Do not argue but pay! The clergyman: Do not argue but believe!" As with the Scotchman and the Hibernian, the participants in Kant's scene speak according to traditional, loud, and familiar modes. The realm of enlightened public discussion is imagined as a negative alternative to all the circulating sounds of authority: "by the public use of one's own reason I understand that use which someone makes of it *as a scholar* before the entire public of the *world of readers*."[12] Print, for Kant, provides circulation beyond the smaller world figured by the shouting officer, tax official, and clergyman. Those echoing sounds provide a productive image of "the way things are now." This image is abstract enough to suggest a powerfully different vision of arguments and counterarguments echoing among people and moving like the scholar who "enjoys an unrestricted freedom to make use of his own reason and to speak in his own person."[13] Strikingly, Kant uses the same figures that midcentury British newspaper writers used to characterize public speech. For the newspaper writers, however, in their focus on day-to-day politics, the world of circulating discourse among multiple figured publics remained central. The possibility of a further abstraction, a concept of unaffiliated, rational, enlightened discussion, remained implicit.

Such implicit possibilities are suggested, again negatively, in a letter published in the *London Chronicle* for August 6, 1765. The writer argues that "the evidence of facts is the only foundation on which men of sense and candour rest their judgment. The whisper of the court, the clamour of the street, the lie of the news-paper, and the sophistry of the pamphlet, go for nothing." The concept of a group of "men of sense and candour" who make careful judgments founded on "the evidence of facts," is constructed here in opposition to the more familiar and local spaces and languages I have been describing. The "lie of the newspaper" is equated with the whisper of the court and the clamor of the street. Orality and print are media associated with particular spaces and conventions. The realm of candor and of facts exists somewhere outside all these spaces and their suspicious modes of discourse. But it can only be described through listing them and then reaching for something more abstract. Unlike them, it is silent. The discussion takes place in the court, in the street, and in print. The realm of facts is where sense and candor can "rest." This rest on a solid foundation is imagined here through grouping images of already abstracted arenas for the circulation of discourse.

This chapter has described a vibrant, growing political culture characterized through images of circulating discourse but quite distinct from the rational discussion and informed public opinion often identified with print culture and political reform. At midcentury, writers imagined a realm of political participation through layered figures, abstracting publics from familiar groupings and languages in the same way that Addison and Steele had abstracted a sociable world from the separate coffee- and tea-tables in the metropolis. A noticeable absence in this chapter has been the term "debate." The letter writers who described the clamor, chat, and applause did not associate it, apparently, with the modes of speech practiced in Parliament or in the great universities. Chapter 4 will explore the usage of the term and argue that debate was treated, like clamor and chat, as a localized, traditional practice from which a public could be figured.

4

Candid Debate: Representing Parliamentary Procedure

IN THE MATERIALS EXAMINED EARLIER IN THIS BOOK, THE TERMS "debate" and "discussion" are noticeably absent. This chapter examines eighteenth-century newspaper reports on debates, in and out of Parliament. Writers used different terms, structures, and forms to describe debates after 1771, when the legal situation made it possible for them to report on Parliament in greater detail. The dramatic differences between representations of debate at different times in the century reveal that debate, like clamor and chat, was figurative. Just as writers used the word "clamor" to suggest an abstracted version of the talk at court, and "chat" to suggest an abstracted version of the conversation around coffeehouse tables, they used "debate" to suggest an abstracted, circulating version of the sort of talk that went on in Parliament. Debate should not be seen as a structure derived from rational rules alone and divorced from local histories and practices. Instead, it is one of several figures used to abstract a general concept of circulating discourse from familiar and local scenes of talk.

We have noted in the earlier chapters that writers describing what a twenty-first-century reader might call "political debate" or "discussion" often avoided those terms, choosing instead to refer to clamor or coffeehouse talk. Debate and discussion play a central role in theories of the public sphere and republican government, where they structure the interactions among members of the public and legitimize concepts such as public opinion and the public good. An informed, mature public opinion is developed, according to such theories, through ongoing discussion among members of the public structured through certain rules and practices: logic, accessibility, empirical evidence. Commentators from John Adams to Elizabeth Eisenstein have claimed that newspapers provided both information to fuel such discussions and a model of anonymous interpersonal interaction to structure them. For this reason, it is important to pay attention to the representations of debate in London's midcentury papers, as well as the absence of the term in places we might expect to see it.

Debates did take place, of course, in Parliament, in the universities, and in clubs, and they were reported upon. The following paragraph, which appeared in the news section of the *London Chronicle* for January 22, 1767, provides a characteristic example of the sort of reporting to be found in newspapers before 1771:

> We hear, that at last Wednesday's meeting of the Society for the Encouragement of Arts, Manufactures, and Commerce; after a certain kind of dexterity had been exhausted to no purpose, in the framing of obstructive questions, to weary people out with debating, (which was almost wholly on the losing side, the other disdaining to make replies, except on the first motion, and every one being carried in the negative by a great majority) the principal question concerning the Land Carriage Fishery, (the pernicious altercations on which long-depending subject had done so much hurt to that very respectable and serviceable Society,) was at length finally decided, at near three o'clock in the morning, in favour of Mr. Blake, by seventy-one votes against sixteen, the tellers included.

The question of the price of fish, and of whether the cost of carrying it overland to market should be subsidized, was discussed in other venues as well.[1] It was an appropriate topic for the Society, founded in 1754, which hosted lectures on science and art with the specific purpose of increasing trade. The idea that the society is "respectable and serviceable" distinguishes it from a coffeehouse club of men meeting only to pass the time. The *Spectator*, reporting on this same meeting, would probably have called it "chat" and would have commented on the characters of the participants rather than the process of reaching the vote or the number of votes on each side. The only such time-wasting talk here is engaged in by the losing side, which "obstructs" the society from its useful work.

Rhetorically, the talk these people engage in is quite different from clamor, as well. It is not addressed the king or his ministers. Instead, it is carried on among the members as they make a decision. The newspaper story assumes that the general public should be interested in this society and in its ideas about the land carriage fishery. This representation of anonymous British people is quite different from those of "A Moderate Man" or "A. Marvel" quoted in chapter 3. Unlike any of the pieces we have read so far, this one positively represents ordinary people talking *to* each other about public policy. This writer reports that the society is using the forms of parliamentary procedure, including motions, questions, and voting, rather than the gossip, compliments, insults, and requests used at court. Just as clamor was appropriated from courtiers by newspaper writers, procedure has been appropriated from Parliament by the members of this society and adopted as well by the newspaper correspondent.

The omissions are also noticeable in this report, however. What, precisely, is the divisive issue about the fishery? Why have the altercations been so pernicious? To decipher this, one would need to know someone in the society. This report rather transparently serves the interests of the winning side and condemns the losers as ineffective and irritating. It implies a set of values favoring consensus, logic, and efficiency, but at the same time refers to a local world of personalities and oral gossip for its context.

London had hosted popular debating societies since the 1730s and 1740s, when the Robin Hood Society met regularly in a pub in Butcher Lane and the Queen's Arms Society in another on Newgate Street.[2] During the seventeenth century, many clubs met, in the city and elsewhere, to discuss politics and religion. Newspaper writers frequently referred to such clubs as a familiar part of social life. The change this chapter will explore was not in the existence of such discussions, but in how their debates were represented and figured in newspapers. Were they local occasions in which individuals met to compete for the approbation of the crowd? Or did they characterize a larger public life? These two ways of representing the discussions of ordinary citizens, I argue, are derived from the language in which newspaper writers represented the debates in Parliament.

One of Parliament's hard-won privileges from the Civil War years was that of meeting in private. It was the king, not the people, from whom Parliament needed to be protected, according to this way of thinking. There was a "gallery" in the House of Commons from which "strangers" could watch the debates, but this was a courtesy on the part of the members, who could and did clear out the gallery when sensitive matters were being discussed. The *Gentleman's Magazine* began publishing accounts of debates in the 1740s. These reports were, however, constructed wholesale from brief notes by hired hack writers, including Samuel Johnson. The preface to a late-eighteenth-century collection of the speeches reconstructed by Johnson clarifies this process: "it is undoubtedly true, that the Parliamentary motions, which are contained in the following sheets, were made, and that they were supported and opposed by the assigned speakers: but, it must be acknowledged, that Johnson did not give so much what they respectively said as what each ought to have said."[3]

Newspapers also published reports on Parliament's debates before 1771, when it was illegal to do so. To get around the legal issue of privilege, they often referred to the debates as if they had taken place in a public debating club, blanked out names, or used nicknames. A news paragraph might report: "it is said an august assembly will very soon make a strict enquiry into the rapid progress of the growth of Popery in this kingdom. . . ."[4] Even in early 1771, writers in the *Public Advertiser* were using these devices. The paper for February 15 includes a reference to "the great Debate on the Spanish Papers," participated in by "Lord B— —," and "Mr. D— —ll." "The Debate lasted till Half an Hour past Three Yesterday Morning, when the House divided; 275 were for the Address, and 157 against it." Other paragraphs mention "the Upper Assembly" and "the Upper Club-Room" when discussing debates in the House of Peers.

Parliament took its privileges seriously. Between 1765 and 1771, eight different printers were arrested for printing accounts of its deliberations. In each case, the printer argued that there was such a large market for this kind of news that his business would suffer if he did not provide it. Appearing before Parliament in 1771, Henry Baldwin of the *St. James's Chronicle* claimed that omitting the debates "would be attended with the Ruin of his Paper." T. Wright, of the *Whitehall Evening Post,* explained that he printed debates "at the instance of several Applications from his Customers in the Country."[5] Newspaper reports on Parliament's debates were so popular in the City that the Lord Mayor Brass Crosby, in whose jurisdiction the arrests of printers were made, began prosecuting the messengers from the House of Commons who came to make the arrests. He claimed they were neither constables nor peace officers of the City and thus had no legal role in making arrests in his jurisdiction. The House of Commons then called Crosby himself to attend and explain his actions. The seriousness of public support for printers and for reports on the House's debates can be seen in newspaper reports on Crosby's appearance in the House: "A prodigious crowd of the better sort were at the Mansion House and in the streets near it, who testified their approbation by repeated huzzas, which were continued quite from the Mansion House to the House of Commons. On his arrival there, one universal shout was heard for near three minutes; and the people, during the whole passage to the House, called out to the Lord Mayor as the People's Friend, the Guardian of the City's rights and the Nation's Liberties."[6] The crowd's political participation is represented in this report according to the sort of "universal shout" figure used by "A. Marvel" and the other writers examined in chapter 3. This crowd met, however, to support printers who were providing news items figured upon different scenes: parliamentary debate rather than universal applause. Crowd action eventually extended to breaking up Lord North's chariot, burning effigies of the princess dowager, Lord Sandwich, and the attorney general among others. Members of Parliament elected from the City, along with Lord Temple, the Marquis of Rockingham, and several other peers, supported the printers. In the face of such resistance, Parliament backed down. According to George Rudé, "the Commons, in spite of their display of authority, suffered a total loss: not only did the defiant printers go unpunished, but the newspapers went on or resumed printing debates, and the House, fearful of stirring up another hornet's nest, had to accept the accomplished fact."[7]

As reports on Parliament's debates included more and more detail, writers moved from reporting almost exclusively on the participants' oratory to focusing more and more on the group's procedures. The two interests are combined in the following report, which appeared in the *Public Advertiser* for November 15, 1770. The writer gradually drops the pretense that the debates took place in the Robin Hood Society:

> On Tuesday the Robin-Hood Debates commenced for the Winter Season; when both the Upper and Lower Societies were extremely full. The former transmitted, as usual, some Propositions to the latter, which being read by the Chairman, were afterwards largely and lamely expatiated upon by Mr. Greville, from whom little could be heard, or understood, except a Motion for the Thanks of the Society for the above Propositions. He was seconded very audibly, in the sermonizing Way, by Mr. Ap-Rice. Considerable Objections, however, to these Thanks were raised on the other Side of the Room, particularly by the great Performer Mr. Barry, who poured forth his Eloquence for above an Hour, by the Glass; in the Middle of which a Thunder-Storm broke forth that almost shook the Room; but happily a Calm soon succeeded. In the Course of this Oration much Freedom was taken with a certain Insinuation, that a late hostile proceeding was the Act of the Governor of Buenos Ayres. He desired to be informed if it was certain that this Governor had acted from his own Motion, and not from the Instruction of the Court. . . .
>
> But one Mr. North, upon whom the Artillery of the Day had powerfully

> fallen, answered very deliberately the Objections that had been made, without returning any of the Fire.[8]

The individuals in this report exchange "fire" in a martial contest characterized by oratorical and meteorological thunder. Although some details of policy and evidence are raised, such as what instructions had been received by the governor of Buenos Aires, the report is structured by the dramatic contest between the administration of Lord North and the opposition led by Isaac Barré.

The debate presented here is more personal and oratorical than rational and enlightened. Like the report on the Society for the Encouragement of Arts and Manufactures, this account assesses the skill of the performers and the approbation of the audience as much as it reports on issues or arguments. The next paragraph comments that "Tuesday Mr. Burke and Colonel Barré convinced the Members of a certain great Assembly, that they were as firm in the Cause of Freedom as ever, by their animated Attack upon the unaccountable Proceedings of the Premier, who was observed several times *to turn pale and gnaw his nether Lip.*" Burke and Barré are here performing for the newspaper-reading audience, and Lord North is represented as both speechless and guilty.

In pre-1771 parliamentary reports, political talk was most often represented and evaluated as oratory. In an account of a libel trial, the *Public Advertiser* for July 19, 1770, reported: "Mr. Thurloe, the Solicitor General, in the Absence of the Attorney General, *who is not ill,* aggravated the Charge in a very bitter, heavy, and dull speech. . . ."[9] The attorney general's absence is interpreted here as disapproval of the proceedings. Since a newspaper printer was on trial for publishing letters critical of the king and administration, the newspaper report is understandably hostile to the prosecution. Thurloe's speech is criticized not for being illogical or innacurate, however, but for being dull. In contrast, "the Solicitor having ended his Harangue, . . . Serjeant Glynn arose, and in a very able Speech explained his Conduct in Almon's Affair, and refuted almost every Argument that Mr. Thurloe had advanced on the Subject. The Serjeant shone much in his Speech, and toward the End was particularly animated in his Sentiments and Expressions. His Hands, till now quiescent on the Head of his Cane, corresponded with his Words: His every Look, and every Action, convinced the Court, that he was really in Earnest,—really inspired with the noble Enthusiasm of Liberty." Later the writer adds that Glynn's "frequent Use of the Term 'proposition,' demonstrates, that he has been conversant in the Study of the Mathematics." Newspaper writers presented the performances of embodied, emotional, and historical individuals to their readers in these reports. The references to earnestness and enthusiasm here suggest that the writer is drawing upon the language Jay Fliegelman identifies as "democratic eloquence," an oratory of sincerity.[10] The speaker's body corresponds with his words because of his sincerity, indicating the virtue of his political positions; they come from the heart, not from his obligations. Other oratorical terms can also be found in newspaper reports, which often reproduced a particularly striking turn of phrase or bon mot, and even reported upon the House's laughter and applause.

Such comments on the agonistic, performative aspects of Parliament's debates can also be found in private letters from the period. Edmund Burke told a correspondent in 1762 that in the House of Lords "Lord Hardwicke spoke very nonsensicially, and in every respect, both of manner and matter, wretchedly . . . Ld Mansfield with his usual dexterity; Lord Bute for two hours; The ministerial people, say admirably. Ld Halifax above par.—In the House of Commons Pitt spoke three hours and twenty five minutes . . . very tedious, unconvincing, heavy, and immethodical."[11] Comments on the debate are framed around the skill of the debaters, although they also break down along party lines; the administration's supporters claim that Bute spoke well and Burke disagrees. Since correspondence was likely to be opened, letters often used the same devices newspapers employed to avoid mentioning individuals and issues specifically. We can find Burke writing to another correspondent with careful vagueness very similar to the newspapers': "to your Enquiry, concerning some Propositions in a Certain assembly of a nature injurious to Ireland, since your departure, I know none of that kind. . . ."[12]

Members of Parliament were prepared for their work by the competitive Latin declamations central to the curriculum at Oxford and Cambridge. Knowledge, fluency, and memory were valued and commented upon by listeners, and gossip about performances circulated among friends and relatives. In a letter to a friend, Lord Holland proudly described one of his son's speeches: "I am told that few in parliament ever spoke better than Charles did on Tuesday—off-hand—with rapidity, with spirit, and such knowledge of what he was talking of as surprised everybody in so young a man. If you think this vanity, I am sure you will forgive it."[13] Commenting on a speech by Sir Ralph Payne the same day, Horace Walpole wrote derisively that "in a pompous oration [he] abused the supporters of the Bill of Rights, protesting on his honour that his speech was not premeditated, but forgetting part, he inadvertently pulled it out of his pocket in writing."[14] Oratorical skill is equated, in such comments, with courtly ease, rather than rational efficiency.

These debates are not the sort characterized by Kant in which participation is defined by the freedom to use one's reason. The powerful and attractive aspect of the public sphere as described by Kant and Habermas is its accessibility and imperviousness to rank, influence, and wealth. Structuring a discussion not around the desires and habits of families and neighbors but around the ideas and analyses of strangers makes it possible to imagine states open to social change, new ideas, and just policies. Such a concept makes it possible to imagine large groups, such as modern states, interacting constructively and without violence, although the individuals within them have no traditional or affective connections to each other. Michael Warner has focused on this aspect of the public sphere in his emphasis on a public as a set of relations among strangers. For Habermas, such a public is imagined through discourse; people become part of the public through participating in rational argument. As an alternative to the embodied, performative, traditional oratory in the above accounts, we might expect to find writers evaluating the logic and evidence of arguments made during debates. In this way, we would be able to identify newspapers' role in the change from an aristocratic to a modern concept of the state. It is, however, very difficult to find midcentury newspaper writers using such terms. As we saw at the end of chapter 3, these writers come closest to Kant's vision of the public when they project a negative space of certainty, defined against the multiple figures of discussion drawn from coffeehouse and court.

Habermas' concept of the public is extremely abstract; all bodies, histories, emotions, and localities are bracketed and all legitimacy is derived from concepts such as law, the market, and rationality. Only the most rigorous thinker can remain in such a mode during the whole of an argument, particularly a political one. Such abstractions lack the metaphorical connection to particular scenes that we have noticed in the other chapters of this book. Rather than basing their accounts of debate on an ideal of such unconstrained rationality, midcentury newspaper writers created figures of circulating talk based on familiar scenes just as they did with clamor and coffeehouse chat. Two scenes of talk were used as the basis for these figures. As we have seen, the first was oratory. The second, as we will see, was procedure. As printers fought a series of legal battles with Parliament over the right to report on the debates, writers included more and more details about motions, questions, committees, and votes. And as reports on Parliament's debates included more such detail, so did reports on debates among other assemblies.

The importance of procedure to reports on Parliament's discussions can be seen in a report from the *Public Advertiser* for Feburary 13, 1771. The "D. of R." is reported to have spoken in the "upper room" of a debating club. Frequent readers would be able to read past these devices, understanding that the upper room was the House of Lords and the D. of R. was the Duke of Richmond. The duke had commented on the tense situation caused by a conflict with Spain over the Falkland Islands. Spain appeared, in early February, to be backing down. The duke:

> expatiated largely on the great Abuses committed by the supposed Necessity of impressing Seamen, especially when we have no prospect of a War; that having upwards of 30 000 Men already in the Service, . . . it became an Object of an Adm— —n who loved Englishmen, to take off as speedily as convenient all the Difficulties under which our own Seamen (some of the most useful Body of the Community) now laboured, that therefore he moved, "that an humble Address be presented to his Majesty, that as his Majesty has accepted a Declaration from Spain for the Injury done to the Honour of his Crown [in invading the Falklands], he will be graciously pleased to give Orders for recalling the Warrants for pressing Seamen and Seafaring-men, a Practice which nothing but Necessity can excuse, as being highly inconvenient to the Trade of this Kingdom, and bearing hard on some of the most useful Orders of his Majesty's Subjects."

This report presents some of the duke's oratorical power in its stylized locutions: "an administration who loved Englishmen," "a practice which nothing but necessity can excuse," and the various references to honor and usefulness. In addition, however, the writer clarifies the duke's use of the forms of parliamentary procedure to make his point. The duke knows that a representative of the ministry will be in attendance and will have to respond to his proposal. He makes a motion to send an address to the king who, with his ministry, negotiates treaties and makes war. His proposal on the topic of impressment, then, will produce a policy statement from the ministry.

The newspaper report also includes the policy statement this tactic produced, although with fewer details: "[Stopping impressments] was vehemently opposed by Ministry, who declared it was no Time to relax whilst we were uncertain whether the K. of S. would ratify [a treaty then being negotiated] and that France and Spain continued to arm at all Points without any Abatement." This debate turns out to be not just about impressing seamen but about the ministry's policy in the negotiations with Spain. By bringing up the issue of impressment, the duke is forcing the minister to articulate his position on Spain and its intentions. Readers can follow the whole debate in the paper. The writer also instructs his readers on how to interpret the ministry's actions: "And thus they gave up the pretended Assurances of an honorable Accommodation." The treaty being negotiated was not strong enough, in the eyes of many British people, to uphold the honor of the nation, which had been insulted by Spain's move. The writer's editorial comment shows not only his sympathy with this position but with the duke's ploy for making the situation clear.

As parliamentary reports grew longer and longer in the years after 1771, moving from a position among other news paragraphs to their own section of many papers, from a paragraph or two to several columns, they included both longer accounts of speeches made by the members and more details about points of order and procedure. By 1774, a frequent reader of newspapers would know about motions, questions, readings, tabling, divisions (votes), and the roles of the speaker and the representative of the ministry. Safe from prosecution, printers allowed writers to name names, to quote directly, and to explain which bills were read, which were tabled, which questions were brought, and who benefited from each. Frequent newspaper readers saw so many reports on addresses like the one the Duke of Richmond proposed, as well as on motions, questions, speeches, and votes, that those procedures became devices as familiar as chat or clamor.

The incorporation of procedural information into reporting on parliamentary oratory can be seen in a piece published April 20, 1774 in the *Public Advertiser.* The title announced "Colonial Barre's Speech on Lord North's Motion for Leave to bring in a Bill, empowering a Governor in North America to send any Officer, who should commit Murder in the Province, to another Colony, or to England, to be tried." Part of the government's reaction to events in Boston, this bill was intended to save British officers from lynching in the event of their being required to face rioting crowds.

Barré's speech takes up three columns and is addressed to the speaker of the house. It begins by claiming that North and his allies have not followed procedure in introducing the bill:

> Upon the present Question I am totally unprepared. The Motion itself bears no Sort of Resemblance to what was formerly announced. The noble Lord and his Friends have had every Advantage of Preparation. They have reconnoitered the Field, and chosen their Ground. To attack them in these Circumstances may, perhaps, favour more of the Gallantry of a Soldier than of the Wisdom of the Senator.
>
> But, sir, the Proposition is so glaring; so unprecedented in any former Proceedings of Parliament; so unwarranted by any Delay, Denial, or Perversion of Justice in America; so big with Misery and Oppression to that Country, and with Danger to this—that the first Blush of it is sufficient to alarm and rouze me to Opposition.

The first few lines of the speech in its newspaper form address parliamentary procedure. Barré accuses the group proposing the bill, those allied with the administration and Lord North, of having introduced the bill too quickly. He is claiming that the ministers have been working in secret, hoping to carry through this measure while Parliament and the people are looking the other way (a claim frequently made by opponents of powerful ministers). Barré makes this claim by calling upon "precedent" and upon "former proceedings of Parliament." The repeated intensifiers "so glaring . . . so unprecedented . . . so unwarranted . . . so big with misery . . ." connect these procedural points to the larger policy points Barre wants to make. The procedural points are given as much rhetorical weight as the policy points, because they relate to a common fear that ministers are practicing statecraft and secrecy. Barré also manages to show off his oratorical mastery through this procedural discussion by claiming that he is speaking without preparation. As we saw in the comments on oratory above, speaking with rapidity and apparent spontaneity combined with knowledge was highly valued in the House of Commons.

The paper's readers could find out from such reports not only what happened in the privileged houses of Parliament, but how it happened. They could learn how this bill was brought and, in a more general sense, how to comment on how a bill is brought. This way of reporting represents political talk as procedural and part of a parliamentary process. Rhetorical convention, ritual combat, and personal dislike were probably all at work in Barré's speech. But parliamentary procedure was also at work, and the newspaper story about the speech made all those aspects available to readers. The newspaper account is not just a representation of oratory, as practiced at Eton and Oxford and in Parliament. It is a representation of a speaker making use of rules that the whole group recognizes to make his point. Precedent and the forms for announcing and introducing a bill are as useful to Barré as his military metaphors and his elegantly parallel syntax. Such procedural details became, for newspaper readers and writers, a formal device for representing speech that was part of a reciprocal, deliberative process.

In his sympathy with the Americans, Barré shared a point of view with many of the writers for the *Public Advertiser*. Benjamin Franklin was contributing letters to the paper at that time. The same column in which Barré's speech was reported included a paragraph commenting that "it was observed that Lord North trembled and faultered at every Word of his Motion for bringing in a Bill to subject America to Military Government." Later in the column a paragraph is devoted to the observation of "a correspondent" that "it is manifestly the Intention of Administration to drive the Americans into actual Rebellion. . . ." In reporting on this speech, however, the *Public Advertiser* did not affect the House's decisions. Pro-American ideas were not widespread in Britain at the time. Barré got very little support in the House, where the opposition was divided. Lord North was secure in his office. But the speech as reported in the paper did add to some of its readers' sense that they understood those actions and the procedures through which they were taken.

This interest in parliamentary detail extended far past the speeches of individual members on politically tense topics. It was customary by 1774 for papers to publish lists of committee reports, bills read and tabled, adjournments, and other procedural details. On February 23, 1774, for instance, the *Public Advertiser* had this account of the House of Commons:

> The House of Commons broke up Yesterday at Half past Four o'Clock, having agreed to the Report of the Resolutions of Monday on the Supply.
>
> Resolved to go into a Committee this Day, to consider of the Exportation of Pease, &c. to Newfoundland.
>
> Ordered a Committee to consider of the Acts relative to the general Turnpike Roads.
>
> Received the Report from the Select Committee on the Jamaica Freeports, and came to a Resolution that the Continuance of the Free-ports of Jamaica is beneficial to the Trade of this Kingdom.
>
> Adjourned to this Day.

The exportation of peas and the beginning of a committee on turnpike roads are less stirring issues than riot and lynching, even for the politicized readers in the City of London or the colonies. Many of these sentences report not on actions taken but on procedures followed: the formations and reports of committees, votes on reports, plans for later in the week. Such news appeared frequently in the papers. In March of the same year, for instance, we find a detailed account of the debate on a bill intended to improve navigation on the Clyde and to build a bridge over it: "Lord Frederick Campbell made a motion, 'That this bill, with amendments, be read a second time now. Mr. M'Doual said he should move for an amendment that the word 'now' be left out, and in the room be inserted 'this day four months.' This occasioned a debate of near three hours."[15] As we will see below, their language influenced reporting on groups outside Parliament as well.

Along with the details of procedure, these reports present exchanges between individual members: Barré and North, M'Doual and his opponents. As they presented more and more detail in their reports, newspaper writers moved from framing Parliament's work as a series of individual speeches to framing it as a series of debates. These detailed reports provided scenes of political talk that could be turned into figures for circulating discussion, as we saw with coffeehouse talk and courtly clamor in the previous chapters. Unlike oratory and clamor, parliamentary procedure and debate provided models for political talk *among* members of a group. In oratory, a single figure addresses a unified group. In clamor, a unified group addresses a single figure. Neither term could help a writer imagine one member of a crowd discussing policy or ideology with another. Coffeehouse talk could do so, but as we saw in chapter 3, it was usually associated with leisure and irrelevance by English writers. Reports on parliamentary debates presented models of exchange in which arguments were traded and exposed to question, where evidence was analyzed, and where oratory and procedure were mobilized as part of an ongoing process of deliberation.

On May 13, 1773, for instance, the *London Chronicle* reported on a debate upon the question of "whether the assay bill for Birmingham and Sheffield would be committed for the next day." Speakers made complex arguments about the possible effects of various policies upon people who committed frauds with weights and measures. John Sawbridge was "entirely against this bill, on the very principles, and for the very reasons, which are urged in its favor. The Honorable Member who spoke last, has pointed out frauds that are committed at London: This is the very reason for confining it to London; for if frauds happen where they are guarded against with so much care—where the officers have ample salaries . . . how much more likely will they be in places where they will not be half so well secured?" Sir George Savile replied that "the Hon. Member who spoke last, has really so confounded the argument, that I scarce know what to think or believe; for I would wish the house would mark the light into which he has thrown it. The Hon. Gentleman behind me (Mr. Gilbert) pointed out the frauds in the office at London. Oh! Says the worthy Alderman, if frauds are committed *here:* it is proof enough they will be committed *there.* . . ."

This passage could be described as a dialogue. In it, characters with recognizable speaking styles are involved in an exchange. It is not the first dialogue we have examined in this study, but it differs from the conversation between Bute and "the mean man" discussed in chapter 3 or the polite exchanges found in the *Spectator* or in courtly diaries. Both speakers refer to logic and evidence as sources of legitimacy: Sawbridge uses an if-then statement and a list of conditions, and Savile questions his interpretation of those conditions. This is starkly different from a representation of what "everyone is saying," as in clamorous complaint, grateful applause, or leisurely chat. These speeches are attributed to individuals who claim to rest their arguments not upon the size of their followings but upon their interpretations of the available evidence.

Such arguments did not, of course, spring upon the English scene suddenly in 1771. Rational argument and the interpretation of evidence can be found in and out of Parliament in all eras. The change this passage exemplifies is in the reporting itself. This newspaper represents the exchange as available and of interest to a large and unidentified readership. A political position is, in the context of such a report, not a finished and unified thing that one group or another has, but a conclusion that can be reached through deliberation and exchange. When the representatives of various clamors and applauses claimed that they were reporting on what they had heard in the West End and the City and the provinces, among all sorts and conditions, they claimed legitimacy for their positions on the basis of the circulation of those positions. This report suggests instead that a political claim might circulate on the basis of its legitimacy. Readers could judge arguments for themselves, interpret the evidence, and participate in a form of the exchange this writer represented. If the position gained adherents, it would be through multiple judgments and interpretations.

Is this a rational public sphere made possible by print? The piece does rhetorically address a reader who can "make public use of reason" in Kant's words, and who sees "the authority of the better argument," in Habermas's. Another newspaper report commented positively on such acts of exchange and interpretation in a debate about a the nature of a bill related to a tontine, or annuity plan: "Mr. O'Neill, who, in the early part of the debate, had spoken warmly against the motion, now rose up, and with a noble candour, declared he was convinced by the arguments of the Speaker, that it was a money bill; and he voted accordingly."[16] Such reports are rhetorically structured by "public" concepts: general access to arguments, the legitimacy of reason, and the social values Habermas sums up with the word "tact," which allow speakers to treat all participants in an argument as equals.

Although these parliamentary reports share many qualities with the public sphere identified by these two writers, they retain their attachment to a specific place, Parliament, and to its history. They do not represent "public discussion"; they make particular discussions public. They imply a conception of political talk among anonymous, ordinary people through access to and imitation of Parliament's discussions. Like coffeehouse talk and clamor, such political talk could be imagined to circulate through imitations of the talk carried out in a specific, familiar, and traditional location. Such talk derived significance from its figurative relation to that specific location. In midcentury papers, "debate" became one more figure to be juxtaposed with those already in use: clamor and coffeehouse talk.

The figurative nature of reports on parliamentary debate can be seen in the effects of those reports on accounts of extraparliamentary groups. On January 12, 1775, for instance, the *London Chronicle* filled several columns with a detailed report titled, "A Circumstantial Account of the Proceedings of the North American Merchants, held last Wednesday at the King's Arms Tavern, Cornhill." These merchants traded with North America and had been hurt by the nonimportation agreements that Americans had entered into in response to the Boston Port Act and Massachusetts Government Act of 1774. These merchants were not members of City government, but they followed a similar form of meeting and deliberation, and they had a similar interest in getting the national government to respond to commercial interests. The paper describes a debate about sending a petition to the king, to explain that the "very extensive trade" between Britain and America "was hurt by the several revenue bills affecting North America, passed since the repeal of the stamp act to the year 1773. [The petition] concluded by praying redress in these particulars, as well as in the operation of all other acts which may affect the general trade carried on between this country and North America." The report ends with the decision that "the petition . . . should lie at that House [the King's Arms Tavern] for signing; and that the Committee should afterwards advertise the meeting at large, of the day they intended presenting it." Rather than merely reporting this result as it might have done in 1765, however, the paper uses two columns describing a "very long, yet an able and candid debate" about whether or not to mention to the Quebec Act in the petition. The Quebec Act, which granted Catholic Canadians religious toleration and French laws and incorporated the entire trans-Appalachian American West into Quebec, was perceived by Americans and their friends as an attack on their interests, because it would surround them with Catholics and possibly create destructive tariff policies.

Mr. Watson is quoted on "the very great constitutional, as well as commercial evils resulting from that bill," which "should be marked out; that he saw no reason why so extensive a province as Canada, the trade whereof was so very material to the interest of this country, should be left out of so great a question as the present; he therefore proposed a clause, after 'the operation of all other acts' 'particularly specifying the late Quebec bill.'" The newspaper writer here, like the one who reported on Barré's speech, gives the reader both Watson's reasoning and his strategy. He proposes an amendment to the petition. His opponents' reasons and strategies are also described: "Mr. Baker answered Mr. Watson, by 'first calling the recollection of the Gentlemen present to the general wish thrown out last meeting, of the Committee's avoiding everything that was political in the petition; he said that they had, in consequence, been very guarded in this particular; but however, be as extensive as they could with prudence, they had still left an open by the words, 'the operation of all other acts.'" By avoiding the "political" questions of particular bills, and their sponsors, in Parliament, Mr. Baker hopes to present this petition to the king as from a group of people interested only in trade. What the newspaper writer has done by giving so much attention to Mr. Watson's proposal is to record the fact that the group actually is political, while at the same time recording their claim that they are not. Such flexibility was one of the many advantages of using the rules of order, both for carrying on the meeting and for reporting on it: "This debate continued several hours, in which Mr. Watson and Mr. Baker were principals on different sides. At the close of it Mr. Watson wanted to put his question; but Mr. Baker set the company right in point of order, by reminding them there was an original question before them, which must first be disposed of." Parliament's rules of order come from ancient precedent. This group is new, but is choosing to abide by rules modeled on those of Parliament. Following these rules seems appropriate in this piece because the talkers and the writer act as if it is appropriate to do so. But it is not a natural way to behave. Other groups at other times have found other ways to organize their work, to achieve consensus, and to arbitrate disputes. By endorsing the rules of procedure, the reporter makes his piece look transparent, like an objective reporting of what happened rather than like an endorsement of the group's vision of itself as reasonable and public.

Both the participants in the meeting and the reporter who attended were imagining, or figuring, this ideal of free debate. If the writer had represented the talk he heard as chat or noise or even popular clamor, he would not have included the details of points of order, of voting, or of amendments that were never adopted. We would have an account of leisurely chat or clamorous murmuring, rather than of Mr. Watson's concerns and Mr. Baker's arguments. By calling it "decent," "manly," "able," and "candid" the writer distinguishes this talk from chat and from clamor. It is different from the *Spectator*'s representation of political talk in its assumption of consequence. These people take themselves seriously despite their plain last names and their apparent lack of court information. Their discussion is assumed to be important because their trade is important. Their talk is more than chat or meddling; it is more consequential. These speakers are taking care of their own business. At the same time, their talk is not modeled on clamor. It does not claim the writer's or the readers' attention because of its volume and repetitiveness, but because of its good order and because of the "great trust" involved in trade.

It is important to recognize the extent to which the work done by newspaper stories like this one was figurative. As political strategy, such activities and their publication had great limitations. The British government was not organized around responding to this kind of argument, no matter what form it took. In the end the North ministry did not repeal any of its revenue bills or the Quebec Act. All the way through the American Revolution, the British government consistently thought in terms of sovereignty and taxes rather than in terms of trade and prosperity, despite the many arguments from merchants, both British and American, suggesting the importance of latter. Despite these problems, however, this newspaper story and the others like it did not question the importance or utility of such deliberations.

I have emphasized the formal aspects of this news story so strongly because they allow the story to seem transparent, without form. It claims to be an objective report of what happened at a committee meeting. But the forms of quotation, summary, and reporting the writer uses allow him to call upon ideals of objectivity and discussion. In the 1770s, as parliamentary reports appeared in greater length and more detail, so did reports of other meetings: the freeholders of Boston (*London Chronicle,* December 15, 1772, reprinted from the *Boston Gazette*), the proprietors of the East India Company (*London Chronicle* September 22, 1772), and the various debating societies and civic associations.

Among the flash points for extraparliamentary political activity in the 1760s and 70s were John Wilkes's arrest for libel in 1763 under a General Warrant and his expulsion from Parliament in 1768 after he had been elected as a City representative from Middlesex. His supporters wrote frequently to newspapers and spoke up in the meetings and clubs formed to protest the government's actions. Historians have followed these developments carefully: "The most important of the societies primarily political in their purpose were, besides the Supporters of the Bill of Rights, who met at the London Tavern, the Sons of Freedom who met at Appleby's tavern in Westminster, the Society which met at the Standard Tavern, Lincoln's Inn Fields, and the long-established Society of the Antigallicians whose annual meeting was said in 1771 to be 'the most numerous meeting of the year of the Middlesex Freeholders.'"[17] Newspapers commented extensively on all these activities, and members of City government reciprocated by protecting printers when they were called before Parliament for libel or breach of parliamentary privilege. Like the members of Parliament, more humble debaters in City government and associations were memorialized in the papers making use of rules of order, presenting addresses to the king, raising motions and questions, and voting on them.

In an interesting collection of newspaper reports on popular debating societies, Donna Andrew claims that from "the smaller disputing clubs" of the 1730s and 1740s, there was an "increase in size and number in the metropolis" until "in 1780 these now enlarged clubs were transformed into large-scale, commercial events, whose managers used the publicity that the burgeoning press sold to advertise their topics of debate, and to combine an expanding interest in public speaking with the respectable pursuit of profit."[18] These comments suggest that there is a difference between the empirical history of debate and the representation of that debate in the newspapers. Andrew claims that the clubs increased in size and number in the 1770s, just as parliamentary debate became a figure available for imparting significance to debates that were already taking place and in some cases had been for thirty or forty years. The language for size, number, circulation, and significance comes from the figures for publicity we have been following in this study. Describing such conversations as widespread, repeated, and circulating is describing them as representative and comprehensible, like coffeehouse talk or clamor. The commodification of debate, by proprietors who charged admission and by newspapers who reported the results, created bourgeois institutions for profiting from discourse figured on state-sponsored and traditional forms, in this case parliamentary debate.

In his study of the press and politics in the eighteenth century, Bob Harris also notes the increase in the number of extraparliamentary bodies whose deliberations were reported in newspapers in these years, particularly in the provinces. He notes "the increasingly sophisticated ways in which traditional bodies—for example, town councils, county meetings, grand juries, as well as other local groups—and individuals sought to exploit provincial papers," Christopher Wyvill being the best example.[19] This increase in sophistication, I argue, was made possible in part by the figurative language that allowed writers and readers to imagine parliamentary procedure and candid debate as circulating and significant discourses.

Not all newspaper writers approved of the activities of such extraparliamentary groups. Proministerial writers frequently parodied the self-importance of the supporters of Wilkes and the officials of the City of London who so frequently claimed to be fighting for the liberty of all Englishmen. These parodies, like the reports above, grew longer and more detailed through the 1770s. They continued to use allegorical figures of the sort presented in the *Spectator,* but employed the literary techniques of formal realism to represent them and their speech.

It is worth examining these parodies in detail, despite their political quietism and apparent indifference to the growth of the middle class, merchant capitalism, and representative democracy in these years. The real intellectual work done by all the writers examined in this study was imagining the political significance of circulating discourse. That work was done through representing several familiar scenes of talk as multiple and interconnected. By juxtaposing those representations, newspaper writers later in the century indicated a condition of discourse more abstract and more significant than any of the particular scenes from which the figures derived. In these parodies, we can identify the various figures of coffeehouse talk, popular clamor, and parliamentary debate, juxtaposed. We can see that their juxtaposition is productive, even if it does not produce political ideas we might find attractive or a concept of the public sphere unfettered from localities and histories.

"Panurge," for instance, commented on an argument over procedure in a letter printed the *Public Advertiser* on November 16, 1770. Using a conventional opening, he claims to have overheard two men arguing in a coffeehouse about how to respond to Parliament's continued refusal to accept Wilkes as a member. Wilkes had been elected three times by the borough of Middlesex, but Parliament expelled him each time and finally chose someone else.[20] Well-organized campaigns against these actions had produced a startling number of petitions to the king on Wilkes's behalf from nearly 50,000 freeholders and citizens of cities and towns.[21] Panurge parodies these petitioners by picturing them bickering over whether to "send instructions to parliament" or "a remonstrance to the King." Such a decision can only be discussed in the language of deliberation and procedure. A clamoring people, by contrast, cannot discuss among its members the form of its expression. Clamor itself is the form, and it is directed upward, not inward.

Panurge's use of the terms associated with debate and procedure is interesting because his portrait of the deliberations is not a sympathetic one. Taking the name of Rabelais's character who always decides that "no" means "yes," this writer portrays the argument over political strategy as a silly squabble, asking, "what does it signify whether a set of raggamuffins meet together to instruct the Parliament, or Remonstrate to the King? They are equally Raggamuffins in both cases, and will be equally disregarded." Although Panurge ridicules the idea that these men are talking among themselves about political strategies, as he does so he represents their political talk in a way that letter writers a decade earlier did not. Ragamuffins or not, these characters were circulated in the *Public Advertiser,* disagreeing about the effectiveness of creating one document or another—a procedural issue. This figure was juxtaposed with coffeehouse talk and clamor as writers argued for and against the importance of City elections. "Cinna" wrote in the same paper: "the [voters in the City of London], God help their weak . . . Heads, make such a Rout and Clamour about the choice of City Officers, as if not only the Fate of this Kingdom, but even that of Europe, depended upon the Election of this or that Mechanic to fill the Chair of Alderman for Billingsgate."[22] Although his figurative language derives ultimately from courtly politics, and he denigrates the status and intelligence of the voters, Cinna's clamor is quite different from those we heard in chapter 3. It is a clamor *among* the voters, not directed from them to someone above them. Such a concept is representable through juxtaposing figures of circulating sound with figures of debate.

Cinna's piece responds to the paper's extensive coverage of the election, which concluded with a piece in the same issue reporting that Richard Oliver had been elected alderman for Billingsgate. Two extensive paragraphs are given to Oliver's speech, and all participants are referred to by their titles (Oliver, an "Esq.," succeeded "the Right Hon. William Beckford, Esq."). Oliver is quoted as saying that the job of alderman is becoming more and more important: "we are struggling for our dearest Inheritance, for those Laws and Liberties which our Ancestors have transmitted to us. In this struggle, which has often returned, the Citizens of London must ever be foremost. . . ." Although their political opinions differ, the writers who lampoon City elections collaborate with those who report on them in developing a concept of public discussion by juxtaposing figures of multiple publics.

A writer who fully exploited the potential of these juxtapositions sent a series of letters to the *London Chronicle* in the summer of 1774, signed "Young Slyboots." Claiming to have just returned to England after a long stay in Lapland, the writer parodies the political scene through a disingenuous naiveté. In the first of these pieces, Slyboots is introduced to a political club in the City by "Deputy Swallowell," "a very intelligent man in the Political World." The members are, Swallowell explains, "some of the most consequential people in the city; wealthy, substantial tradesmen, men of sound understanding, and deep penetration; we punctually meet once a week, not merely for the sake of enjoying social conversation, but to preserve the Constitution." This is a similar group of people to the American merchants—City tradesmen and merchants, doctors, bourgeioses. Like the merchants, they meet to talk politics, and they claim great importance for their endeavors. But Young Slyboots's parody uses different forms for representing the meeting. Rather than parliamentary procedure, he uses allegorical figures similar to the *Spectator*'s "Abraham Froth," engaged in leisurely coffeehouse talk. Framed in this way, the meeting is a display of self-importance and excess rather than a process of achieving practical aims. In claiming to be able to preserve the constitution, Swallowell reveals not his responsibility and candor but his self-importance and obtuseness. Even his praise of his own punctuality suggests an out-of-balance sense of his consequence.

In representing, through dialogue, the characteristic talk of City merchants and politicians, this writer calls upon the tradition of dismissing political interest as meddling and chat. He represents the talk in such detail, however, that his writing involves itself in the very questions it deplores as unimportant for people like his subjects and presumably many of his readers. The club meeting begins with the report of "Mr. Deputy Blamange," who is asked by the chairman whether he found any "inconvenience from yesterday's business":

> I wish I could say I had not, Mr. Chairman (replied the Deputy, coughing) for I am afraid I shall be laid up again with the plaguy gout. Such a confounded jumble over the stones is worth a West India government. I don't mind going up with an address on the birth of a prince of a fig, because besure we do then get some excellent caudle and cake, and I can sometimes pocket a bit for my little girl; but really, Mr. Chairman, it is dearly earning five shillings to go up with a remonstrance from Guildhall to St. James's, and all the way back again, without once eating or drinking.

Like the tens of thousands of freeholders and citizens who had participated in the movement to petition in favor of Wilkes's seat in Parliament, this club participates in taking petitions and instructions to the king's court at St. James's. Mr. Blamange, however, would rather make the rough ride over the cobblestones from Guildhall, the seat of the fractious government of the City, to St. James's for a congratulatory "address" than a protesting "remonstrance." Unlike Mr. Watson and Mr. Baker, or the aldermen for Billingsgate, these speakers are not represented as vessels for the refining of ideas through rational debate. Instead, they are appetites, for both food and importance. Mr. Blamange, who is presumably a pudding in more than name, takes his duty of bringing the people's ideas to their government as a chance to earn five shillings and to perhaps get some food. The writer shows that Mr. Blamange's engagement with such endeavors has made him "a little swelled with a sense of his own importance." His cough, his gout, and his greed all suggest that he is an appetite on legs rather than a rational being.

Like Cinna's letter above, however, this piece involves itself in the very details it claims to find irrelevant. The differences between an instruction, a remonstrance, and an address were serious in both procedural and policy senses. Addresses were much more closely linked to applause and clamor and were comprehensible as expressions of grateful subjects recognizing traditional hierarchical relations. Instructions and remonstrances, however, made claims upon the state's representative nature that, in the era of American responses to the Stamp Act, were much more politically unsettling.

Mr. Blamange, named allegorically and employed parodically, speaks in dialect and moves physically through a landscape in a style approaching the novelistic. By figuring this discussion as one of many debates happening around the city, and including some of the familiar forms of those debates, this writer invests the circulating and general aspect of coffeehouse talk with the detailed and substantive nature of debate. Even in parody, this piece participates in imagining political discussion as a phenomenon of multiple, juxtaposed, circulating discourses.

Mr. Blamange is succeeded by an even more grotesque character:

> Mr. Deputy Paunch, who sat immediately on my right hand, and added much to my uneasiness, being so immoderately corpulent, I could not look at him without fancying him in the most imminent danger of bursting; he really appeared choaked with excessive fat, not being able to speak but with great difficulty through his throat, which always gave pain to those who heard him, who expected every moment to see him throttled. One of the Members told me, "it was a misfortune greatly to be lamented, for that in other respects Mr. Deputy Paunch has great oratorical talents; but his want of facility and volubility of speech (continued this discerning Member) is amply compensated for in the strength of his understanding, and the wisdom of his observations, which in my opinion are superior gifts of nature."

Mr. Paunch's body is so overwhelming that it almost chokes off his speech, making him the complementary opposite of a rational committeeman who can speak in the paper because he so ably represents the disembodied public. Paunch is ridiculed for his silence, which Mr. Spectator so frequently claimed as a virtue. He is unable to speak because he is overwhelmed by his own body and presumably, like Mr. Blamange, by his appetites. Unlike the party writers examined in chapter 3, who saw sound itself as a symptom of political problems and wished for silence, Slyboots here calls upon a concept of rationality and virtue opposed to particular bodies and desires that could be taken straight from Habermas. Deputy Paunch and Mr. Blamange are ridiculous in these passages not because they are debating at all but because their debate is not sufficiently candid.

The most detailed dialogue in the piece comes with the arrival of

"Mr. Coniac, the little Patriotic Printseller, whose face I think was studded with the finest sort of carbuncles I ever beheld." He:

> fanned his face, and drank a bumper of Brandy to prevent his catching cold, the Chairman ventured to accost him thus: "Well, Mr. Coniac. you was there to-day I suppose?"—To which he replied, (with a strong emphasis) *"I was"*—"well, and did you see him?"—"I did," (returned Mr. Coniac)—"you saw him did you?" (rejoined the Chairman) "and pray how did he look? how did he appear?—The Members all seemed eager to hear Mr. Coniac, who rising slowly from his seat, with great deliberation replied, "I saw him come from the Drawing Room with Lord North laughing!"—Ha! cried some.—"I say I saw him laughing!"—"Then (said the Chairman shrugging up his shoulders) you find that Mr. Alderman Harley was at Court to-day and actually was seen to laugh with Lord North: now Gentlemen are the Citizens to be made Papists or not?"—Upon this a hum and a buzz went around the room; the Members looked wise at each other, and resumed their pipes, and I did not hear Mr. Coniac speak again the whole evening.

This dialogue stands in direct opposition to City people's depictions of themselves as representative members of the public. It includes stage directions ("with a strong emphasis," "rising slowly from his seat") again suggesting that this is a physical scene, rather than a battle of abstract ideas. The content of the conversation is precisely the sort of information traded at court in order to orchestrate clamor effectively. The dialogue is a narrative in which repetition builds tension until the truth is revealed, but the trivial nature of that truth allows the writer to ridicule the whole situation. The club members are trading court information, even as they claim to safeguard the constitution. Like the *Spectator,* Young Slyboots represents coffeehouse politicians as wasting time and overestimating their own importance by interfering in things outside their own family and neighborhood. Like the *Spectator,* Young Slyboots uses narrative, dialogue, and setting to champion moderation by criticizing excess. But his dialogue, which distinguishes the various speakers, lends more drama to their relations with each other and to the details of their arguments. By juxtaposing the familiar and conventional tropes of coffeehouse talk and courtly clamor with figures for candid debate, this writer treats detailed political discussion as a familiar, circulating, and significant social phenomenon, even as he parodies the citizens of London for engaging in it.

Unlike the *Spectator,* which was reluctant to enter into such details, this parody gives a detailed, though hostile, description of how the increasing influence of City government was expanding the networks through which court information and the views of interest groups might pass. The City government did take remonstrances to St. James's. The newspaper pieces assume that the reader has knowledge of these events and personalities and provides more to those who do not.

In another piece written for the *London Chronicle,* Slyboots claims he has overheard John Wilkes and John Reynolds whispering a box in the Chapter coffeehouse. Wilkes points out that "the Society [for the Supporters of the Bill of Rights] was formed solely for the discharge of my debts" and refuses to allow any of the money to be spent on a City election. He claims that it was good to have run a losing candidate for a city position because "it was much better than suffering the election without any opposition, for nothing can be more fatal to us than a calm." Wilkes did resist the use of the society's money for anything but paying his own debts.[23] The newspaper letter, then, provides context for news paragraphs elsewhere in the paper and engages other writers who claim that Wilkes represents the liberties of all Englishmen.

In the conversation Slyboots claims to have overheard between Wilkes and Reynolds, they discuss a candidate who, despite their support, has lost an election for sheriff. Wilkes says "it was rash and absurd to put up men who (however subservient to our purposes) were Aliens in the City, in opposition to persons of Character and Property, and who were esteemed by the Public." In this way the piece takes a position on a particular city election and upon political strategies and policies. Unlike the court-oriented political writers discussed in chapters 2 and 3, these writers ignore the relative virtues of the ministries in and out of power and concentrate on how to address them. The issues at stake in these pieces circulate among people outside the government: is Wilkes really a good representative? How effective are the remonstrances sent by City government to the king? Parliamentary debate, in its procedural form, provides a model for imagining political conversation and a form for representing political dialogue that was unavailable to A. Marvel ten years earlier. Both the parodies and the detailed accounts of meetings, unlike the representations of talk in newspapers in the 1760s, represent members of the public talking to and disagreeing with each other about politics, rather than speaking with a single united voice or babbling incomprehensibly.

Both the report on the meeting about the Quebec Act and the Slyboots pieces preach against the dangers of excess. Slyboots is explicit about this: "the Reader, however, must not imagine, from the account I have given of this Weakly Club, that it was entirely composed of staunch Patriots, for I soon perceived that some of the Members were not hearty in the Cause, and that others were but lately initiated, and not quite broke in. Indeed some even presumed, now and then, to speak of Politics with moderation, which caused their conduct to be narrowly watched." Slyboots argues for moderation by ridiculing excess, and by claiming that the group polices itself to produce only excess. The merchants piece makes the same argument by showing how the merchants are able to discuss their differences with candor and to resolve them. The process itself refines extreme positions by subjecting them to criticism from others. All these writers describe "the people" not as readers, but as talkers. The question is what kind of talkers they are. As writers on one side began to make frequent use of procedure and detail, writers on the other made frequent use of dialogue and dialect. A printed argument about the nature of City politics, then, was created by writers who juxtaposed figures of discourse as general and circulating. Coffeehouse talk, courtly clamor, and parliamentary debate provided figures of physical spaces, social practices, and familiar vocabularies that were imagined as general, circulating, and significant in their relations to each other. An accessible, abstract, ongoing sphere of public discussion was created by the juxtaposition of multiple figures of more local and limited conversations.

Discussing this period in the history of periodical publishing, John Klancher refers to a "'society of the text' in an eighteenth-century sense." Writers at midcentury, he argues, addressed a public they imagined as unified. This imagined unity would fraction as British readers and writers responded to events on the continent and to conflict at home over labor and the franchise. In later periodicals, he sees instead a "'polity' of the text which presupposed other, competing polities."[24] We can read midcentury newspapers and the other texts that surrounded them as engaged in a project of assembling such a "society of the text" out of multiple texts and multiple gestures of association, abstraction, and substitution.

The very unity of the eighteenth-century public sphere that critics of Kant and Habermas have found so suspicious was created out of juxtaposed, layered, and repeated figures of multiple exchanges in multiple spaces. "The clamour of the people" is distinct, in important ways, from the demands of radical workers discussed by Klancher and from the "entire public of the *world of readers*" invoked by Kant. The people imagined, represented, and addressed in midcentury papers achieved unity and singularity through multiple layers of figurative language: tropes upon tropes. If they were an imagined community, that imagining was no single projection of fraternity or rationality outward to national borders. Instead, it was achieved through an accretion of metaphors based on oral, manuscript, and print texts and on court, coffeehouse, and parliamentary spaces.

Epilogue: Figurative Publics and Revolutionary Discourse

If juxtaposed figures of circulation and publicity structured the language of newspaper reporting on politics at midcentury, what happened in 1789? in 1793? This epilogue suggests ways in which attention to figures and the relations between figures might influence our reading of political discourse from the era of the French Revolution.[1] It is clear that the British response to events in France made political debate both more polar and more rigidly surveilled. In the debate between Edmund Burke and Thomas Paine, for instance, one way in which this separation happened was through eliminating juxtaposition. Burke's figures derive their metaphorical resonance from orality; Paine's derive from print. Unlike the newspapers we have been examining, in which figures from print, manuscript, and orality jostle one another on a page and even within a column, Burke and Paine organize and rank their images. Each imagines a nation structured around a particular form of circulation and a particular scene of interaction. Each vision of the present and future is thus unified, compelling, and incommensurate.

Thomas Paine argues in the terms we have come to associate with the enlightenment, the spread of print culture, and the bourgeois public sphere. He claims that reading spread ideas through the populations of America and France, changing those countries utterly. His metaphors are consistently visual, picturing truth as a text that appears to all, needing only light to circulate it among populations: "such is the irresistible nature of truth, that all it asks—and all it wants,—is the liberty of appearing. The sun needs no inscription to distinguish him from darkness; and no sooner did the American governments display themselves to the world, than despotism felt a shock and man began to contemplate redress."[2] Paine makes "inscription" on manuscript paper or stone monuments a debased form of writing that requires endorsement by a patron. It is made irrelevant by the truth that, like the sun or a newspaper, is available to everyone as long as it has the liberty to appear in print.

Earlier, in *The Crisis,* Paine associated the points for which he argued with the natural order and with science, in enlightenment terms: "Here, in this spot is our own business to be accomplished, our felicity secured. What we have now to do is as clear as light, and the way to do it is as straight as a line."[3] Geometry, optics, and logic are assumed here to reveal inarguable and natural truths which, once they "have the liberty of appearing," spread through a population and cause action. Paine associates this clarity and circulation with print in his comparison between the American, French, and British constitutions in *The Rights of Man.* He ridicules Britain's "unwritten" constitution and Burke's defense of it by comparing it to America's, which is printed and circulated: "Here we see a regular process—a government issuing out of a constitution, formed by the people in their original character; and that constitution serving, not only as an authority, but as a law of control to the government. It was the political bible of the state. Scarcely a family was without it. Every member of the government had a copy; and nothing was more common, when any debate arose on the principle of a bill, or on the extent of any species of authority, than for the members to take the printed constitution out of their pocket, and read the chapter with which such matter in debate was connected." Printedness, here, is equated with circulation—every family has one—and with authority. Like the qualities of a straight line or a ray of light, these qualities of printedness are assumed. Paine does not explain why it is that printing conveys authority upon a text or how he knows that rays of light are as straight as lines. All these associations, as Adrian Johns and Michael Warner have demonstrated, were built slowly by printers and scientists over the course of the early modern period and only came to be assumed through the work of writers such as Paine. In his usage he erases the contingency of these associations; it is their very obviousness that invests print images with persuasive power.

In contrast to America's printed, circulated, authoritative constitution, Paine describes the British constitution as a product of the orality through which the British state does its work: "The continual use of the word Constitution in the English Parliament shows there is none; and that the whole is merely a form of government without a Constitution, and constituting itself with what powers it pleases. If there were a Constitution, it certainly could be referred to; and the debate on any constitutional point would terminate by producing the Constitution. One member says this is Constitution, and another says that is Constitution—To-day it is one thing; and to-morrow something else—while the maintaining of the debate proves there is none. Constitution is now the cant word of Parliament, tuning itself to the ear of the Nation."[4] Sound, unlike light, is changeable, seductive, and fashionable, according to the set of terms Paine develops here. Unlike the American constitution, which can be produced from a legislator's pocket to provide authority, the British constitution is "cant," fashionable jargon produced to create a pleasant "tune," fooling the nation into accepting Parliament's actions. Using the same association Erin Mackie identifies in the *Spectator,* Paine assigns these qualities to orality: "I cannot believe that any nation, reasoning on its own rights, would have thought of calling these things a constitution, if the cry of constitution had not been set up by the government. It has got into circulation like the words bore and quoz [quiz], by being chalked up in the speeches of parliament, as those words were on window shutters and doorposts. . . ."[5] His own use of fashionable words, bore and quoz, again distinguishes the changeable nature of spoken language, or language written in chalk, from the authoritative printed page, circulated among legislators and families, and self-evident whenever light falls upon it.

Paine's claims about the nature of the reading public have structured our conceptions of it ever since. It is surprising, in this context, to see how far Paine departs from the language of the daily newspapers we associate with the development of print culture. Reading Paine in the context of the midcentury British newspapers examined earlier in this study, we can see that the printed objects that served so well as a vehicle for his metaphors did not actually use such language themselves. He, and other republican writers such as John Adams and Benjamin Franklin, grasped and exploited the capacities of print for imagining one kind of public.[6] But we misread their work if we see it as an empirical description of the development of print culture. Looking at the political writing newspapers actually carried reveals the intellectual distance these writers traveled as they imagined print republicanism, and it also reveals the possibilities of the alternate, multiple publics that they strategically ignored.

I do not mean to argue here that print republicanism had no empirical existence. It is clear that the British government believed in Paine's critical public as an empirical reality, because of the steps taken to crack down on it. And the corresponding societies, debating clubs, and radical movements of the late eighteenth and early nineteenth centuries did use print as a technology and as a concept for furthering their work. It is when such writers project their histories and imagine their universalities that they choose selectively among the many metaphors available in the discourse around them. Reading with attention to the uses of these metaphors can help us understand their work as writers at the same time that it can help us imagine alternatives to their metaphorical polities.

Burke's *Reflections on the Revolution in France* can be seen drawing upon the figures that Paine omits. Full of clamor and complaint, the book projects a modern public as an abstracted version of a historical feudal scene, and it celebrates that projection. The printed texts Paine describes as authoritative and truthful, such as the publications of the British Revolutionary Society, are described by Burke as unsupported by oral credit: "I never heard a man of common judgment, or the least degree of information, speak a word in praise of the greater part of the publications circulated by that society." Using "information" in the sense we saw in chapter 2, and making the authority of a printed text subject to words spoken in praise or blame, Burke condemns the Revolutionary Society in the language of clamor. Within a frame of reference where importance is measured by volume of sound, he dismisses Richard Price and his associates by pointing out that "until lately, I do not recollect to have heard of this club."[7] Rather than vessels of the truth that can be seen by anyone as long as the light falls upon it, he describes them as an unsuccessful party, attempting to create a clamor but without the connections to create enough echoes: "several petty cabals, who attempt to hide their total want of consequence in bustle and noise, and puffing, and mutual quotation of each other."[8] Even the printed writing of the revolution's sympathizers is recast here as noise and as ineffective noise. All political interactions, in Burke's picture of the current state of things, are imagined through images of the nation as a series of circles surrounding the scenes where influential conversations are conducted.

Burke rests authority upon familiarity with oral modes of interaction as consistently as Paine derives it from light on a printed page. Describing his own authority, Burke writes: "I speak from the experience I have had in a pretty extensive and mixed communication with the inhabitants of this kingdom, of all descriptions and ranks, and after a course of attentive observation, began early in life, and continued for near forty years."[9] He claims that his authority comes not from self-evident truth, but from mixture, and not from a decontextualized printed page, but precisely from context: he has moved around the kingdom and spoken (and presumably written and read) with people of all descriptions and ranks. His references to print have quite different associations: "We [the British people] have not been drawn and trussed, in order that we may be filled, like stuffed birds in a museum, with chaff and rags, and paltry, blurred shreds of paper about the rights of man."[10]

Note that there is a further mixture that Burke ignores—the mixture of metaphors based on oral, manuscript, and printed sources, and court, coffeehouse, and parliamentary scenes that we saw in the newspapers examined in this study. His "mixed communication" is not so mixed that it partakes of the juxtapositions we saw in the *London Chronicle* and *Public Advertiser*. He separates images of print, associated with ephemerality and refuse, from images of orality, associated with communication and experience. Rather than the suggestive juxtapositions of A. Marvel and Old Slyboots, we see in Burke a ranked, ordered, and unified set of images deriving their power from the tradition for which he argues. Part of this difference, of course, derives from genre. A four-hundred-page book by a single writer will usually be more unified than a newspaper written by many writers and assembled by a printer. In both Burke and Paine, however, the consistency with which figures of publicity are ordered and ranked derives from their projects of enlisting readers in a vision of polity organized around a single source of authority.

A public imagined through multiple, juxtaposed figures of interaction is less rigorous, but also more familiar, flexible, and accessible than a public modeled entirely on the distancing and decontextualized aspects of print or the traditional and deferential aspects of talk. Even "public debate" itself draws upon a metaphor based on a single mode of interaction and thus reduces the range of possible publics. Eighteenth-century British political writers suggested many more possibilities through their juxtaposed figures, even if they did not exploit them all. They were fond of claiming that they lived in the freest nation in the world, a place where everyone read and everyone talked about politics. The following examples of this claim are drawn from writers with differing political interests: [A newspaper is] "a bill of fare, containing all the luxuries, as well as the necessaries of life. *Politicks* are now the *roast-beef* of the times, and a dish equally sumptuous to the king and the cobbler." "This kingdom, from those of the highest station down to the very lowest class, is divided into two cabals; one is angry with the government, and the other displeased with those who are not angry with it. To be silent on this head makes a man be looked on as a mere idiot, not capable so much as to reason on state affairs, or politics, as it is called here." "Without newspapers . . . our country Villager, the Curate, and the Blacksmith, would lose the self-satisfaction of being as wise [as] our First Minister of State." "In a land of unlimited freedom, where every man from the Prince down to the Cobler is a politician, it is not to be wondered at that much should be said and wrote which has no tendency to make one either wiser or better."[11] As the negative tone of some of these comments shows, such claims do not imply that British writers imagined themselves and their fellow-citizens engaged in rational debate, modeled either on the Roman Forum or the printed page. Instead, as we have seen, these claims referred to a conglomeration of conversations, letters, and printed documents, imagined as clamor, coffeehouse chat, and parliamentary declamation and procedure; each one amplified, echoing, and circulating among citizens and subjects.

Notes

Introduction

1. Michael Warner, *Letters of the Republic: Publication and the Public Sphere in Eighteenth-Century America* (Cambridge, MA: Harvard University Press, 1990); Adrian Johns, *The Nature of the Book: Print and Knowledge in the Making* (Chicago: University of Chicago Press, 1998); Margaret Ezell, *Social Authorship and the Advent of Print* (Baltimore: Johns Hopkins University Press, 1999); Harold Love, *The Culture and Commerce of Texts: Scribal Publication in Seventeenth-Century England* (Amherst: University of Massachusetts Press, 1998); and Adam Fox and D. R. Woolf, eds., *The Spoken Word: Oral Culture in Britain, 1500–1700* (Manchester, Manchester University Press, 2002).

2. Horace Walpole, *Horace Walpole's Correspondence,* ed. W. S. Lewis, Warren Hunting Smith, George L. Lam (New Haven: Yale University Press, 1954), 10:274.

3. Joseph Addison and Richard Steele, *The Spectator,* ed. Donald Bond (New York: Oxford University Press, 1965), 1:127. All further references are to this edition.

4. *Spectator,* no. 1, 1:3.

5. Geoffrey Holmes and Daniel Szechi, *The Age of Oligarchy: Pre-Industrial Britain 1722–1783* (New York: Longman, 1993), 201.

6. *London Chronicle,* September 24, 1765.

7. Michael Warner, *Publics and Counterpublics* (New York: Zone Books, 2002), 86.

8. Benedict Anderson, *Imagined Communities: Reflections on the Origin and Spread of Nationalism,* revised edition (New York: Verso, 1991).

9. Jürgen Habermas, *The Structural Transformation of the Public Sphere: An Inquiry into a Category of Bourgeois Society,* trans. Thomas Burger and Frederick Lawrence (Cambridge, MA: MIT Press, 1992), 33–35.

10. Nancy Fraser, "Rethinking the Public Sphere: A Contribution to the Critique of Actually Existing Democracy," in *The Phantom Public Sphere,* ed. Bruce Robbins for the Social Text Collective (Minneapolis: University of Minnesota Press, 1993), 3, 9.

11. Jeremy Black, *The English Press in the Eighteenth Century* (Philadelphia: University of Pennsylvania Press, 1987), 115.

12. Hannah Barker, *Newspapers, Politics, and Public Opinion in Late Eighteenth-Century England* (Oxford: Clarendon Press, 1998), 76, 77.

13. John Brewer, *Party Ideology and Popular Politics at the Accession of George III* (New York: Cambridge University Press, 1976); E. P Thompson, "Eighteenth Century English Society: Class Struggle without Class?" *Social History* 3 (1978); and George Rudé, *Wilkes and Liberty: A Social Study of 1763 to 1774* (New York: Oxford at the Clarendon Press, 1962).

14. Kathleen Wilson, *The Sense of the People: Politics, Culture and Imperialism in England, 1715–1785* (New York: Cambridge University Press, 1998).

1. Figuring Coffeehouse Talk

1. Brian Cowan, "Mr. Spectator and the Coffeehouse Public Sphere," *Eighteenth-Century Studies* 37, no. 3 (2004), 345–66; Erin Mackie, *Market a la Mode: Fashion, Commodity, and Gender in the Tatler and the Spectator* (Baltimore: Johns Hopkins University Press, 1997); Scott Black, "Social and Literary Form in the *Spectator*," *Eighteenth-Century Studies* 33, no. 1 (1999), 21–42; and Tedra O'Sell, "The Ghost-Writer: English Essay Periodicals and the Memorialization of the Public in the Eighteenth Century" (PhD diss, University of Washington, 2002), 38–42.

2. "Anti-fashion fashion" is Mackie's term. *Market a la Mode,* 5.

3. Cowan, "Mr. Spectator," 352–53.

4. Mackie, *Market a la Mode,* 7.

5. Jürgen Habermas, *The Structural Transformation,* 16.

6. Mackie, *Market a la Mode,* 4.

7. Ibid., 5.

8. Michael Warner, *Letters of the Republic,* 66–67. Habermas, *Structural Transformation,* 42.

9. J. G. A. Pocock, *The Machiavellian Moment: Florentine Political Thought and the Atlantic Republican Tradition* (Princeton: Princeton University Press, 1975).

10. Cowan, "Mr. Spectator," 358.

11. Warner, *Letters of the Republic,* 64.

12. Cowan, "Mr. Spectator," 360, Warner, *Letters of the Republic,* 66.

13. S. Black, "Social and Literary Form," 28. Black refers to *spectator* #435, which discusses "irregularities" such as "every absurd fashion, ridiculous custom, or affected form of speech." 4:27.

14. Addison and Steele, *The Spectator,* 1: 180–81.

15. Pocock, *Machiavellian Moment,* 450.

16. Habermas, *Structural Transformation,* 33.

17. Steve Pincus, "'Coffee Politicians Does Create': Coffeehouses and Restoration Political Culture," *Journal of Modern History* 67 (December 1995), 834.

18. O'Sell, *Ghost-Writer,* 37.

19. Mackie, *Market a la Mode,* 5.

20. Pocock, *Machiavellian Moment,* 456.

21. "Imagined Community" is Benedict Anderson's term, and "public sphere" comes from Habermas. Anderson, *Imagined Communities.* 6–7.

22. Hugh Blair, *Essays, Lectures on Rhetoric and Belles Lettres* (London: W. Strahan and T. Cadell, 1783) 408–9.

23. December 11, 1762. James Boswell, *Boswell's London Journal,* ed. Frederick A. Pottle (New Haven: Yale University Press, 1992), 76.

24. July 25, 1765.

25. An asterisk explains that the reference to grinding razors "alludes to the Razor-Grinder's Ballad, at Sadler's Wells."

26. *London Chronicle,* October 17, 1765.

2. Creating a Clamor

1. Habermas, *Structural Transformation,* 32.

2. James, 2nd Earl Waldegrave, *The Memoirs and Speeches of James, 2nd Earl Walde-*

grave, 1742–1763, ed. J. C. D. Clark (Cambridge: Cambridge University Press, 1988), 176.

3. Horace Walpole to George Montagu, Tuesday June 8, 1762. *Horace Walpole's Correspondence,* 10:35.

4. Waldegrave, *Memoirs and Speeches,* 215.

5. John M. Beattie, *The English Court in the Reign of George I* (Cambridge: Cambridge University Press, 1967), 10, 16.

6. Beattie, *English Court in the Reign of George I,* 5, 6.

7. Waldegrave, *Memoirs and Speeches,* 181.

8. Ibid.

9. Warner, *Publics and Counterpublics,* 86.

10. Habermas, *Structural Transformation,* 7.

11. Ibid., 23–24.

12. Walpole, *Horace Walpole's Correspondence,* 30:128.

13. Warner, *Publics and Counterpublics,* 96.

14. William James Smith, ed. *The Grenville Papers: Being the Correspondence of Richard Grenville, Earl Temple, K.G. and The Right Hon.: George Grenville, Their Friends and Contemporaries.* 3 vols. (New York: AMS Press, [1852]1970) 1:152–53.

15. Walpole, *Horace Walpole's Correspondence,* 30:191.

16. See Smith, *Grenville Papers,* 1:198.

17. Ibid., 1:357.

18. See Holmes and Szechi, *Age of Oligarchy,* Chap. 19.

19. See Thomas W. Copeland, "Introduction" in *The Correspondence of Edmund Burke* (Chicago: University of Chicago Press, 1958), 1:xxi.

20. Burke, *Correspondence of Edmund Burke,* 1:205.

21. Basil Williams, *The Life of William Pitt, Earl of Chatham* (New York: Octagon Books, 1966), 1:174.

22. Walpole, *Horace Walpole's Correspondence,* 30:197.

23. John Hervey, *Some Materials Towards Memoirs of the Reign of King George II,* ed. Romney Sedgwick, 3 vols. (New York: AMS Press, [1931] 1970), 1:128–29.

24. Waldegrave, *Memoirs and Speeches,* 176.

25. The term "oral culture" has been used by Walter Ong and Jack Goody, among others. The critique of their terms by Brian Street focuses on indigenous, working class, and other nonelite speakers and writers and takes quite a different path from the argument I present here. Walter J. Ong, *Orality and Literacy: The Technologizing of the Word* (New York: Methuen, 1982). Jack Goody, *The Interface Between the Written and the Oral* (Cambridge: Cambrige University Press, 1987). Brian V. Street, *Literacy in Theory and Practice* (New York: Cambridge University Press, 1984).

26. Walpole, *Horace Walpole's Correspondence,* 30:185.

27. J. Black, *English Press,* 117.

28. Barker, *Newspapers, Politics, and English Society,* 22. Hannah Barker, *Newspapers, Politics, and Public Opinion in Late Eighteenth-Century England* (Oxford: Clarendon Press, 1998), 77. Other volumes exploring this issue, and placing it in the context of newspaper production and distribution, include Black's *English Press;* Bob Harris, *Politics and the Rise of the Press: Britain and France 1620–1800* (New York: Routledge, 1996); Michael Harris and Alan J. Lee, eds., *The Press in English Society from the Seventeenth to the Nineteenth Centuries* (Madison, NJ: Farleigh Dickinson University Press, 1986); and Robert R. Rea, *The English Press in Politics, 1760–1774* (Lincoln: University of Nebraska Press, 1963).

29. Public opinion did influence political events during the century: protests over excise under Walpole, suspicion of Bute as first minister, and support for Wilkes all had practical effects on state actions. These effects were not achieved through representative structures, however, but through mob and crowd actions, often seen as "complaint" or "clamour." The contemporary understanding of such actions as familiar elements of the traditional social hierarchy is explained in E. P. Thompson, "The Moral Economy of the English Crowd in the Eighteenth Century," *Past & Present* 50 (1971): 76–136. For accounts of popular political life and its relation to virtual representation, see Brewer, *Party Ideology and Popular Politics*, and Wilson, *Sense of the People*.

30. For social and geographical distribution of readership, see Barker, *Newspapers, Politics, and English Society*, 61. Evidence in this study is drawn entirely from London newspapers. Recent work has suggested that newspapers in the provinces, both English and American, differed in significant ways from those in the metropolis. Although provincial editors made up most of each issue from reprints of material from London papers, the selections were often determined by local interests and issues. The language of "we hear" and "clamour" was certainly available and familiar to provincial readers. See Barker, *Newspapers, Politics, and English Society*, 104–14; C. Y. Ferdinand, *Benjamin Collins and the Provincial Newspaper Trade in the Eighteenth Century* (New York: Clarendon Press, Oxford University Press, 1997); and G. A. Cranfield, *The Development of the Provincial Newspaper* (New York: Oxford, 1962); Charles E. Clark, *The Public Prints: The Newspaper in Anglo-American Culture, 1665–1740* (New York: Oxford, 1994), 11.

31. July 25, 1765.

32. J. Steven Watson, *The Reign of George III 1760–1815* (Oxford: Oxford University Press / Clarendon Press, 1960), 102n. Walpole, *Horace Walpole's Correspondence*, 6:323.

33. Lawrence Lipking, *Samuel Johnson: The Life of an Author* (Cambridge, MA: Harvard University Press, 1998), 12–15.

34. *London Chronicle*, August 1, 1765, and August 6, 1765.

35. *Letters to H. S. Woodfall, 1763–1799*, British Library Add 27780. The *Post* had published a letter claiming that Sandwich had tried to sell an admiralty commissioner's post. A jury awarded damages to Sandwich. See Rea, *English Press in Politics*, 220.

36. See Barker, *Newspapers, Politics, and English Society*, 40–41, 104, 106, 112–14, and Black, *English Press*, 35–37.

37. Habermas, *Structural Transformation*, 36.

38. Ibid., 83.

39. Elizabeth Eisenstein, *The Printing Press as an Agent of Change: Communications and Cultural Transformations in Early-Modern Europe*. 2 vols. (New York: Cambridge University Press, 1979); Goody, *Interface Between the Written and the Oral*.

40. See John Fortescue, ed., *The Correspondence of King George the Third From 1760 to December 1783* (London: Frank Cass & Co. Ltd., 1967), 1:104–18, for another view of these events.

3. Clamor in the Newspapers

1. *London Chronicle*, September 21, 1765.
2. Warner, *Publics and Counterpublics*, 116.
3. Horace Walpole, *Horace Walpole's Correspondence*, 30:191. See chapter 2, page 54.

4. Brewer, *Party Ideology and Popular Politics,* 141.
5. Barker, *Newspapers, Politics, and English Society,* 22; Clark, *Public Prints,* 11.
6. Public opinion did influence political events during the century: protests over excise under Walpole, suspicion of Bute as first minister, and support for Wilkes all had practical effects on state actions. These effects were not achieved through representative structures, however, but through mob and crowd actions, often seen as "complaint" or "clamour." For a more complete account of popular political life in the period, see Brewer, *Party Ideology and Popular Politics,* and Wilson, *Sense of the People.*
7. Holmes and Sczechi, *Age of Oligarchy,* 281.
8. Barker, *Newspapers, Politics, and English Society,* 53, 81–83.
9. Rea, *English Press in Politics,* 100.
10. *Public Advertiser,* March 1, 1765.
11. *Public Advertiser,* January 4, 1765.
12. Immanuel Kant, "An Answer to the Question, What is Enlightenment," in *Practical Philosophy,* ed. and trans. by Mary J. Gregor (New York: Cambridge University Press, 1996), 18.
13. Kant, "Answer to the Question," 19.

4. Candid Debate

1. J. Black, *English Press,* 74, quoting from the *Oxford Gazette and Reading Mercury* from June 13, 1768.
2. Donna Andrew, *London Debating Societies, 1776–1799* (London: London Record Society, 1994), vii.
3. Samuel Johnson, *Debates in Parliament.* 2 vols. (London: printed for John Stockdale, 1787), vi–vii. Hannah Barker explains parliamentary reporting in this period: "Between 1703 and 1729, Abel Boyar published parliamentary proceedings in his magazine, *The Political State of Great Britain.* However, to escape prosecution, debates were published some time after they took place and were presented as history rather than news. Charles Knight noted how Edward Cave of the *Gentleman's Magazine* began publishing some from of record of debates at the end of each session in 1736, using only the initials of the speakers, although this ruse had to be made even more covert in 1738, after a resolution of the Commons expressly forbade the practice, and thereafter the debates appeared as those of 'the Great Senate of Lilliput.' The *London Magazine* took similar action and began to report the proceedings of an imaginary club. However, like Boyer's productions, such reporting was always dated. Both publications were called to account in 1747 by the House of Lords for publishing reports of the trial of Simon Lord Lovat for high treason during the Jacobite rebellion of 1745, and Cave then ceased publishing parliamentary reports altogether, although the London Magazine continued to print carefully disguised accounts of a 'political club.'" *Newspapers, Politics, and English Society,* 77.
4. *London Chronicle,* January 17, 1767.
5. Rea, *English Press in Politics,* 206.
6. *Gentleman's Magazine,* 1771, 139–40 and *Middlesex Journal,* March 18–21, 1771, quoted in Rudé, *Wilkes and Liberty,* 160.
7. Rudé, *Wilkes and Liberty,* 165.

8. The paper notes that this passage is reprinted from the *London Packet.* Such reprinting was a common practice at the time.

9. This was the trial "of Mr. Miller, for re-publishing Junius's Letter to the K— — in December last, in the London Evening Post."

10. Jay Fliegelman, *Declaring Independence: Jefferson, Natural Language, and the Culture of Performance* (Stanford: Stanford University Press, 1993).

11. Burke to Charles O'Hara, December 12, 1762. *Correspondence of Edmund Burke,* 1:160.

12. Burke to Henry Flood, May 18, 1765. *Correspondence of Edmund Burke,* 1:193.

13. To Mr. Campbell of Cawdor. Charles James Fox, *Memorials and Correspondence of Charles James Fox,* ed. Lord John Russel (London: Richard Bentley, Publisher in Ordinary to her Majesty, 1853) 52–53.

14. Quoted in Fox, *Memorials and Correspondence,* 52.

15. *London Chronicle,* March 29, 1774.

16. *London Chronicle,* March 17, 1774.

17. Lucy S. Sutherland, *The City of London and the Opposition to Government, 1768–1774* (New York: Oxford University Press, 1959), 19n. Quoting from the *Public Advertiser,* April 25, 1771. Note that it was these same Antigallicians who were described as clamoring and applauding by "Civis" and "A Citizen" in the pieces discussed at the end of chapter 3. The empirical activities of these groups alone were not enough to inspire writers to use the language of candid debate.

18. Andrew, *London Debating Societies,* vii.

19. Harris, *Politics and the Rise of the Press,* 48.

20. See Rudé, *Wilkes and Liberty,* chaps. 6–9.

21. Ibid., 135.

22. *Public Advertiser,* July 5, 1770.

23. Rudé, *Wilkes and Liberty,* 61.

24. Jon P. Klancher, *The Making of English Reading Audiences, 1790–1832* (Madison: University of Wisconsin Press, 1987), 39.

Epilogue

1. Analysis of the British response to the French Revolution is a much larger field than I can fully survey here. This epilogue is intended to be suggestive rather than definitive. I am particularly indebted in my reading to the discussion of the debate between Burke and Paine in Klancher, *Making of English Reading Audiences,* 98–11; and Steven Blakemore, *Crisis in Representation: Thomas Paine, Mary Wollstonecraft, Helen Maria Williams, and the Rewriting of the French Revolution* (Madison: Fairleigh Dickinson University Press), 25–57. My understanding of British writers' interest in drawing a distinction between enlightenment claims to universality and traditional claims of authority was assisted by Zeynep Tenger and Paul Trolander, "The Politics of Literary Production: the Reaction to the French Revolution and the Transformation of the English Literary Periodical," *Studies in Eighteenth-Century Culture* 24 (1995): 279–95; and Andrew McCann, *Cultural Politics in the 1790s: Literature, Radicalism and the Public Sphere* (New York: Macmillan-St. Martin's, 1999).

2. Thomas Paine, *The Rights of Man* (Garden City, NY: Anchor Books, 1973), 394.

3. Thomas Paine, *Common Sense and the American Crisis* (New York: G. P. Putnam's Sons, 1912), 255.

4. Paine, *Rights of Man,* 370.

5. Ibid., 429.

6. I have made this argument about Franklin at more length in "Benjamin Franklin, Writing by Hand: Manuscript, Print, and Political Imagination," *Journal for Early Modern Cultural Studies* 4, no. 2 (Fall/Winter 2004): 89–113.

7. Edmund Burke *Reflections on the Revolution of France* ed. Conor Cruise O'Brien (New York: Penguin Books, 1981), 87.

8. Burke, *Reflections,* 181.

9. Ibid., 180.

10. Ibid., 182.

11. In a letter from "W. C." in *St. James's Chronicle,* July 22, 1780, quoted in Barker, *Newspapers, Politics, and Public Opinion,* 35; *London Chronicle,* August 8, 1765, "From the CHINESE SPY, just published, The Mandarin Cam-pi to the Mandarin Prime Minister at Pekin"; *Lloyd's Evening Post,* 1780, quoted in Barker, *Newspapers, Politics, and English Society,* 17; "J. W." in a letter to the *London Chronicle* for April 12, 1774.

Bibliography

Addison, Joseph, and Richard Steele. *The Spectator*. Edited by Donald Bond. 5 vols. New York: Oxford University Press, 1965.

Anderson, Benedict. *Imagined Communities: Reflections on the Origin and Spread of Nationalism*. Revised edition. New York: Verso, 1991.

Andrew, Donna. *London Debating Societies, 1776–1799*. London: London Record Society, 1994.

Barker, Hannah. *Newspapers, Politics, and English Society, 1695–1855*. Harlow, UK: Longman, 2000.

———. *Newspapers, Politics, and Public Opinion in Late Eighteenth-Century England*. Oxford: Clarendon Press, 1998.

Beattie, John M. *The English Court in the Reign of George I*. Cambridge: Cambridge University Press, 1967.

Black, Jeremy. *The English Press in the Eighteenth Century*. Philadelphia: University of Pennsylvania Press, 1987.

Black, Scott. "Social and Literary Form in the *Spectator*." *Eighteenth-Century Studies* 33, no. 1 (1999): 21–42.

Blair, Hugh. *Essays, Lectures on Rhetoric and Belles Lettres*. London: W. Strahan and T. Cadell, 1783.

Blakemore, Steven. *Crisis in Representation: Thomas Paine, Mary Wollstonecraft, Helen Maria Williams, and the Rewriting of the French Revolution*. Madison: Fairleigh Dickinson University Press, 1997.

Boswell, James. *Boswell's London Journal*. Edited by Frederick A. Pottle. New Haven: Yale University Press, 1992.

Brewer, John. *Party Ideology and Popular Politics at the Accession of George III*. New York: Cambridge University Press, 1976.

Burke, Edmund. *The Correspondence of Edmund Burke*. 10 vols. Edited by Thomas W. Copeland. Chicago: University of Chicago Press, 1958.

Burke, Edmund. *Reflections on the Revolution in France*. Edited by Conor Cruise O'Brien. New York: Penguin Books, 1981.

Clark, Charles E. *The Public Prints: The Newspaper in Anglo-American Culture, 1665–1740*. New York: Oxford University Press, 1994.

Cowan, Brian. "Mr. Spectator and the Coffeehouse Public Sphere." *Eighteenth-Century Studies* 37, no. 3 (2004): 345–356.

Cranfield, G. A. *The Development of the Provincial Newspaper*. New York: Oxford University Press, 1962.

Dean, Ann C. "Benjamin Franklin, Writing by Hand: Manuscript, Print, and Political

Imagination." *Journal for Early Modern Cultural Studies* 4, no. 2 (Fall/Winter 2004): 89–113.

Eisenstein, Elizabeth. *The Printing Press as an Agent of Change: Communications and Cultural Transformations in Early-Modern Europe.* 2 vols. New York: Cambridge University Press, 1979.

Ezell, Margaret. *Social Authorship and the Advent of Print.* Baltimore: Johns Hopkins University Press, 1999.

Ferdinand, C. Y. *Benjamin Collins and the Provincial Newspaper Trade in the Eighteenth Century.* New York: Clarendon Press, Oxford University Press, 1997.

Fliegelman, Jay. *Declaring Independence: Jefferson, Natural Language, and the Culture of Performance.* Stanford: Stanford University Press, 1993.

Fortescue, John, ed. *The Correspondence of King George the Third From 1760 to December 1783.* London: Frank Cass & Co. Ltd., 1967.

Fox, Adam, and D. R. Wolfe, eds. *The Spoken Word: Oral Culture in Britain, 1500–1700.* Manchester: Manchester University Press, 2002.

Fox, Charles James. *Memorials and Correspondence of Charles James Fox.* Edited by Lord John Russel. London: Richard Bentley, Publisher in Ordinary to her Majesty, 1853.

Fraser, Nancy. "Rethinking the Public Sphere: A Contribution to the Critique of Actually Existing Democracy." In *The Phantom Public Sphere.* Edited by Bruce Robbins for the Social Text Collective. Minneapolis: University of Minnesota Press, 1993.

Gay, John. *The Present State of Wit.* London, 1711.

Goody, Jack. *The Interface Between the Written and the Oral.* Cambridge: Cambrige University Press, 1987.

Habermas, Jürgen. *The Structural Transformation of the Public Sphere: An Inquiry into a Category of Bourgeois Society.* Translated by Thomas Burger and Frederick Lawrence. Cambridge, MA: MIT Press, 1992.

Harris, Bob. *Politics and the Rise of the Press: Britain and France 1620–1800.* New York: Routledge, 1996.

Harris, Michael, and Alan J. Lee, eds. *The Press in English Society from the Seventeenth to the Nineteenth Centuries.* Cranbury, NJ: Farleigh Dickinson University Press, 1986.

Hervey, John. *Some Materials Towards Memoirs of the Reign of King George II.* Edited by Romney Sedgwick. 3 vols. New York: AMS Press, [1931] 1970.

Holmes, Geoffrey, and Daniel Szechi, *The Age of Oligarchy: Pre-Industrial Britain 1722–1783.* New York: Longman, 1993.

Johns, Adrian. *The Nature of the Book: Print and Knowledge in the Making.* Chicago: University of Chicago Press, 1998.

Johnson, Samuel. *Debates in Parliament.* 2 vols. London: printed for John Stockdale, 1787.

Kant, Immanuel. "An Answer to the Question, What is Enlightenment." In *Practical Philosophy.* Edited and translated by Mary J. Gregor. New York: Cambridge University Press, 1996.

Klancher, John P. *The Making of English Reading Audiences, 1790–1832.* Madison: University of Wisconsin Press, 1987.

Letters to H. S. Woodfall, 1763–1799. British Library.

Lipking, Lawrence. *Samuel Johnson: The Life of an Author.* Cambridge, MA: Harvard University Press, 1998.

London Chronicle. London, England.

Love, Harold. *The Culture and Commerce of Texts: Scribal Publication in Seventeenth-Century England.* Amherst: University of Massachusetts Press, 1998.

Mackie, Erin. *Market a la Mode: Fashion, Commodity, and Gender in the Tatler and the Spectator.* Baltimore: Johns Hopkins University Press, 1997.

McCann, Andrew. *Cultural Politics in the 1790s: Literature,Radicalism and the Public Sphere.* New York: Macmillan-St. Martin's, 1999.

Ong, Walter J. *Orality and Literacy: The Technologizing of the Word.* New York: Methuen, 1982.

O'Sell, Tedra. "The Ghost-Writer: English Essay Periodicals and the Memorialization of the Public in the Eighteenth Century." PhD diss., University of Washington, 2002.

Paine, Thomas. *Common Sense and the American Crisis.* New York: G. P. Putnam's Sons, 1912.

———. *The Rights of Man.* Garden City, NY: Anchor Books, 1973.

Pincus, Steve. "'Coffee Politicians Does Create': Coffeehouses and Restoration Political Culture." *Journal of Modern History* 67, no. 4 (1995): 807–834.

Pocock, J. G. A. *The Machiavellian Moment: Florentine Political Thought and the Atlantic Republican Tradition.* Princeton: Princeton University Press, 1975.

Public Advertiser. London, England.

Rea, Robert R. *The English Press in Politics, 1760–1774.* Lincoln: University of Nebraska Press, 1963.

Rudé, George. *Wilkes and Liberty: A Social Study of 1763 to 1774.* New York: Oxford at the Clarendon Press, 1962.

Smith, William James, ed. *The Grenville Papers: Being the Correspondence of Richard Grenville, Earl Temple, K.G. and The Right Hon.: George Grenville, Their Friends and Contemporaries.* 3 vols. New York: AMS Press, [1852] 1970.

Street, Brian V. *Literacy in Theory and Practice.* New York: Cambridge University Press, 1984.

Sutherland, Lucy S. *The City of London and the Opposition to Government, 1768–1774.* New York: Oxford University Press, 1959.

Tenger, Zeynep, and Paul Trolander. "The Politics of Literary Production: the Reaction to the French Revolution and the Transformation of the English Literary Periodical." *Studies in Eighteenth-Century Culture* 24 (1995): 279–95.

Thompson, E. P. "Eighteenth Century English Society: Class Struggle without Class?" *Social History* 3 (1978) 133–165.

———. "The Moral Economy of the English Crowd in the Eighteenth century." *Past & Present* 50 (1971) 76–136.

Waldegrave, James, 2nd Earl. *The Memoirs and Speeches of James, 2nd Earl Waldegrave, 1742–1763.* Edited by J. C. D. Clark. Cambridge: Cambridge University Press, 1988.

Walpole, Horace. *Horace Walpole's Correspondence.* Edited by W. S. Lewis, Warren Hunting Smith, and George L. Lam. 36 vols. New Haven: Yale University Press, 1954.

Warner, Michael. *Letters of the Republic: Publication and the Public Sphere in Eighteenth-Century America.* Cambridge, MA: Harvard University Press, 1990.

———. *Publics and Counterpublics.* New York: Zone Books, 2002.

Watson, J. Steven. *The Reign of George III 1760–1815.* Oxford: Oxford University Press / Clarendon Press, 1960.

Williams, Basil. *The Life of William Pitt, Earl of Chatham.* 2 vols. New York: Octagon Books, 1966.

Wilson, Kathleen. *The Sense of the People: Politics, Culture and Imperialism in England, 1715–1785.* New York: Cambridge University Press, 1998.

Index

Addison, Joseph, 21, 26, 32, 37
American Revolution, 18, 19, 26, 116, 127
American colonies, 19, 110, 111, 114, 116, 122, 127
Anderson, Benedict, 15, 74, 94, 96
Andrew, Donna, 117–18
Appleby's Tavern, 42

Barker, Hannah, 20, 62
Barré, Isaac, 104–5, 109–11
Bedford, 4th Duke of (John Russell), 63
Billingsgate, 120
Black, Jeremy, 19, 62
Black, Scott, 26, 30
Blair, Hugh, 39
Bond, Donald, 35
Boswell, James, 41
Brewer, John, 77
Burke, Edmund, 56, 57, 65, 105, 106, 127, 130–31
Bute, 3rd Earl of (John Stuart), 19, 45, 47–8, 55, 60–61, 76, 78–82, 90, 106, 113, 136

Charles II, 33
Chesterfield, 4th Earl of (William Dormer Stanhope), 47, 65
Child's coffeehouse, 38, 41
circulation, 14, 23, 36, 37, 39, 41–43, 45–46, 50, 52, 53, 75, 83, 91, 94, 95, 112, 118
City of London, 25, 96, 103–4, 119–24
civic republicanism, 29, 31, 26, 37
clamor, 14, 22, 47, 54–9, 62, 75–77, 81–86, 88, 95–98, 118, 119, 123
Clark, Charles E., 78
closet (king's), 48–49
clubs, 36–38, 120–22
coffeehouses, 11, 14, 15, 22–23, 32–39, 42, 44, 45, 50, 61, 66, 69, 77, 88, 89, 95–96
constitution (American), 128
constitution (British), 120, 128
conversation, 31, 41, 43–44, 59, 66, 68, 95
court, 12, 14, 23–24, 32–33, 36, 46, 51, 53, 60–61, 63, 71–73, 123
Cowan, Brian, 26, 28–30
Crisis, The (Thomas Paine), 128
crowds, 80, 103–4

debate, 14, 23–24, 66, 68, 88, 89, 93, 99, 100, 112, 114–18, 119, 122, 128, 131
dialogue, 97, 113, 122, 125
discussion, 68, 72–73, 74, 83, 84, 88, 89, 98, 100, 114, 120
Drawing Room (king or prince's), 11, 12, 46, 47, 48–50, 54
Dryden, John, 32

East India Company, 117
Eisenstein, Elizabeth, 20, 69, 100
eloquence. *See* oratory
empire, 51, 60, 73

faction, 17, 86, 94
figurative language, 13–14, 23–24, 26, 28–29, 59, 61, 74–78, 83–86, 91, 94, 97, 98, 100, 112, 114, 116, 117–19, 126, 127, 130–31
forum, 37, 42, 47
Fox, Henry (Lord Holland), 52, 53–54, 57, 60–61, 106
Franklin, Benjamin, 111, 129
Fraser, Nancy, 17
Frederick, Prince of Wales, 49–50
French Revolution, 26, 127–31, 138

Garrick, David, 43, 44
George II, 48, 49, 50, 52, 53, 54
George III, 19, 47, 48, 54, 55, 58, 61, 63, 65, 67, 71, 78–82, 84, 119
gossip. *See also information and clamor*, 36, 61, 66
Grafton, 3rd Duke of (Augustus Fitzroy), 63, 73
Grenville, Elizabeth, 53
Grenville, George, 53, 54–55, 57, 58, 60–61, 63–65, 79, 82, 87, 89

Habermas, Jürgen, 11, 16–17, 20, 21, 22, 25, 27, 28, 32, 33, 46, 51, 68–69, 72, 73, 75, 84, 94–95, 97, 107, 114, 125
Hampton Court, 48
Harrington, James, 31, 32
Harris, Bob, 118
Hervey, John, 58–59

imagined community, 37, 74, 97, 126
information (as a term for court gossip), 47, 49, 51–52, 59, 70, 123, 130

Jenkinson, Charles, 54–55, 58, 76
Johns, Adrian, 28, 128
Johnson, Samuel, 65, 102–3
Junius, 87

Kant, Immanuel, 11, 20, 51, 94–95, 98, 107, 114, 124
Klancher, John, 125

letters to the printer, 22, 75, 78–91
levee, 47–8, 62, 67, 69–70, 73
London Chronicle, 12, 14, 18, 25, 62, 63, 71, 73, 76, 77, 78, 86, 88, 98, 101, 114, 117, 120, 123
London Evening Post, 42, 84, 85

Mackie, Erin, 26, 27, 28, 30, 34, 36, 129
mail, 27, 28, 35
manuscript as a medium, 11, 36, 50, 54, 59, 60, 64, 106
Marvell, Andrew, 32, 81
mobs, 79–82, 92–93
"Moralist, The" 14, 43–44

Newcastle, 1st Duke of (Thomas Pelham-Holles), 47–48, 56, 62, 64–65, 79
news, 27, 36, 68, 78
newspapers, 45, 46, 61–70, 74–78 85, 117; advertising in, 86; North American, 78; production and distribution of, 68, 86, 136; provincial, 68
North, Frederick, Lord, 96, 104–5, 109, 111, 123
Northington, 1st Earl of (Robert Henley), 71
Norton, Fletcher, 64

opera, 43–44
orality, 59, 60, 94, 98, 128–29, 135
oral forms as media, 12–13, 50, 59, 60, 74, 79–80, 130
oratory, 41–2, 104–7, 122
O'Sell, Tedra, 26, 33

Paine, Thomas, 127–29
Parliament, 11, 12, 17, 19, 23–24, 34, 46, 49, 58, 59, 77, 83, 89, 100, 129; newspaper reports on, 100, 102–4, 137; Wilkes and, 117, 119
parliamentary procedure, 23–24, 102, 107, 108–12, 115–16, 119–20, 124–25
patronage, 46, 53, 54, 81
Pincus, Steve, 32–33
Pitt, William, 13, 55–57, 63–4, 71, 79, 85, 90–91, 106
Pocock, J. G. A., 28, 31, 34, 37
Pope, Alexander, 26
print as a medium, 12–13, 29, 50, 59, 60, 64, 68, 74, 77, 94, 98, 127
print culture, 11, 12, 68, 99, 113–14
Public Advertiser, 11, 17–18, 20, 42, 70, 72, 83, 95, 103, 104, 105, 108, 109, 111, 119
public, 11, 21, 50, 60, 62, 63, 74, 85–87, 94, 99, 130
public opinion, 11, 62, 67, 74, 78, 81–82, 89, 90, 99, 136
public sphere, 16–17, 21–22, 26, 37, 38, 42, 51, 53, 78, 91, 98–99, 113–14, 125

Rea, Robert, 87
reading audience, 45, 68, 76–77, 83, 85, 87, 94, 125, 129, 136

reason, 11, 16, 26, 66, 68–69, 83–84, 85, 97, 100, 113, 114, 122
representation (political), 77, 83
Richmond, 3rd Duke of (Charles Lennox), 60–61, 108–9
Rights of Man (Thomas Paine), 128
Robin Hood Society, 23, 102, 104
Rockingham, 2nd Marquess of (Charles Watson-Wentworth), 55–56, 63–65, 79, 87, 89, 104
republican government, 11, 24
Rudé, George, 104

Scott, James, 87
Sackville, Lord George, 54, 61
Sandwich, 4th Earl of (John Montagu), 44, 45, 60, 67–68, 87, 104
Seven Years' War, 18–19, 54, 70, 78–80
silence, 94, 98, 85–86, 131
Society for the Encouragement of Arts and Manufactures, 23, 101–2
Society of Supporters of the Bill of Rights, 117, 124
Spectator, 11, 14, 16, 21, 25–45, 88, 96, 101, 113, 116, 118, 120, 123
St. James's, 42, 48, 71, 121
St. James's Chronicle, 103
Steele, Richard, 21, 30, 32, 33, 34, 36
Swift, Jonathan, 95

Tatler, 34
tea-tables, 30, 37, 39, 43, 44
Temple, 1st Earl of (Richard Grenville), 60, 104
"To Any Minister or Great Man," 92–95
Tories, 44
Townshend, Charles, 54, 56

voice, 12, 20, 74, 80, 118

Waldegrave, 2nd Earl of (James Waldegrave), 47, 48–50, 51, 69, 70
Walpole, Horace, 13, 32, 47, 52, 54, 60–61, 76, 106
Walpole, Robert, 58–59
Warner, Michael, 15, 28, 29, 32, 50–51, 53, 57, 75–76, 97, 107, 128
West End (of London), 68, 70
Whitehall Evening Post, 66, 103
Whigs, 29, 44
Wilkes, John, 19, 25, 42, 117, 119, 120, 124, 136
Wilson, Kathleen, 20, 77–78, 88
Woodfall, Henry, 67, 95–96

Yarmouth, Countess (Amalie Sophie Marianne Wallmoden), 52, 53